Edwin Lester Linden Arnold

Coffee

its Cultivation and Profit

Edwin Lester Linden Arnold

Coffee
its Cultivation and Profit

ISBN/EAN: 9783743306301

Manufactured in Europe, USA, Canada, Australia, Japa

Cover: Foto ©Andreas Hilbeck / pixelio.de

Manufactured and distributed by brebook publishing software (www.brebook.com)

Edwin Lester Linden Arnold

Coffee

COFFEE:

ITS CULTIVATION AND PROFIT.

BY

EDWIN LESTER ARNOLD.

AUTHOR OF "ON THE INDIAN HILLS; OR, COFFEE PLANTING IN SOUTHERN INDIA,"
"A SUMMER HOLIDAY IN SCANDINAVIA," &C.

LONDON:
B. WHITTINGHAM & CO., 91, GRACECHURCH STREET.

1886.

PREFACE.

IT was with considerable diffidence I undertook the task of preparing a new handbook on Coffee cultivation. Already many names of weight and authority were down on the roll of those who had gained experience in the wide field of practice, and had recorded in admirable handbooks the results of many years' planting wisdom.

Sabonadière has enshrined his name with the best period of Ceylon Coffee culture; Laborie's works are classical, and still useful; R. H. Elliot's "Experiences of a Planter in the Jungles of Mysore" has thrown a glamour over the industry in the eyes of many an outward-bound "griffin;" Ellis, Hull, Keen, Lewis, Shortt, and Simmond have all contributed treatises of good sense and point on the same subject, thus thrashed over and over again, until a casual observer would deem there was but small chance of any stray grains of fact remaining untouched.

But the truth is, the world moves, and with it its most mundane affairs, not excepting those of Coffee.

What was the view of experts twenty years ago is now as often as not looked upon as antiquated, and fresh demands are continually being made upon science and research for investigation and the fruits of novel discoveries. Then also new districts have been opened up, many deserving that the attention of those interested in this branch of commerce should be drawn to them as supplying fresh fields for enterprise and capital, and changing by their prosperity the face of regions which, though once clothed in dense jungle, are now patched with the luxuriant green gardens characteristic of the industry, and dotted with the white bungalows of European superintendents. To gaze over a tract thus changing hands—from Nature's to men's—is an experience not easily forgotten; the fair and fruitful plantations already won from primeval barbarism lying along the hollows of, it may be, a wild upland valley, surrounded on every side by the swelling masses of forest only awaiting their turn to come under the woodman's axe; a mountain stream winding down the glen, a thread of silver in the dry weather, and a turgid torrent in the monsoon, supplying water for the wants of man and beast, besides motive power for pulping, saw-driving, and all the other hundred wants of a plantation; the long ghaut road trailing away into the distance, with its slow-moving trains of bullock carts or labourers, the populous native huts, and all the many signs of busy active life.

To look down upon such a region, as I have done very many times, bursting into usefulness in the face of great odds, inevitably impresses on the observer a consciousness of the vast amount of wealth and energy constantly devoted to this productive and widespread industry, hinting at the great possibilities that are opening up for its furtherance in new lands, while at the same time explaining the constant demand for works on the subject by both those who supply the motive power in the form of home capital for all such undertakings, and those who go abroad to accept the practical portion of the task.

My enterprising Publishers think there is an opportunity for rendering assistance to both parties by the preparation of a handbook which shall be at once concise and yet full of practical information, equally useful at home or in the hands of the young assistant making his first voyage to the tropics; up to the day in its data, containing the latest figures on production and profits, and hints on every matter, in fact, that can be required by either of the two great divisions of investors in Coffee already mentioned—those who embark capital in it, and those who dedicate their lives and energies to the profession.

The outcome of my task—undertaken with due doubts in my abilities, and carried through with a genuine pleasure born of pleasant reminiscences and a congenial subject—is now before the reader; and that it may prove useful and convey a lucid impression of the "facts and figures" of Coffee cultivation is the chief wish of

THE AUTHOR.

CONTENTS.

CHAPTER		PAGE
I.	The Plant	1
II.	Soil and Climate	19
III.	Labour and Labourers	35
IV.	Purchase	49
V.	The Nursery	58
VI.	Forest Clearings	69
VII.	Pits and Pegs	78
VIII.	"Shade"	87
IX.	Planting	96
X.	Weeds	104
XI.	Pruning	109
XII.	Enemies	117
XIII.	Buildings and Bungalows	135
XIV.	Roading and Draining	153
XV.	The Crop	158
XVI.	Pulping and Preparing	167
XVII.	Cattle and Fodder	185
XVIII.	Manures and Manuring	194
XIX.	Cost and Profit	215
XX.	Coffee Countries	229

LIST OF ILLUSTRATIONS.

	PAGE
BACK AND FRONT VIEW OF BUNGALOW	143
TRANSVERSE SECTION OF COFFEE MILL	170–71
"DISC" PULPER	173
THE COMBINED CRUSHER AND PULPER	174
LONGITUDINAL SECTION OF COFFEE MILL	176–7

COFFEE:

Its Cultivation and Profit.

CHAPTER I.

THE PLANT.

THERE are certain historic facts relating to the cultivation of Coffee, and the introduction of the drink into this country, which are interesting, if not of much practical value, and must receive a brief notice here.

The plant, whose natural climatic range lies between the isothermal lines of 25° North and 30° South of the Equator, is said to have been first observed in Caffa (whence its name), a district of Southern Abyssinia. From thence it was introduced along the old caravan routes to Yemen, in Arabia, about the beginning of the 14th century. There can be little doubt, however, that it has always grown spontaneously in various quarters of the tropics, Persia, Peru, and the West Coast of Africa (whence an important species takes its name) being rivals for the honour of its parentage.

The Medina Sheik Abd-el-Kader is the oldest historical authority on the use of "blood red Keweh," as the Tunisian Ibu Waki named the beverage. It may be assumed that the Coffee Plantations of Yemen increased until the yield served for export as well as for home consumption. In the 16th century mention is made of the consumption of Coffee by the Turks, and Lord Bacon among other writers alludes to it. The Coffee came by ships from Mocha to Suez, and overland by caravans to Damascus and Aleppo, the total export from Mocha in the middle of the 17th century being estimated by Dufour at about 16,000 bales, weighing about 300 lbs. each, *i.e.*, about 2,150 tons. Rauwolfius brought some young plants to Western Europe in 1573, and Alpinus stood sponsor to them, scientifically describing and naming the botanical curiosities in 1591. This seems to have drawn some attention to the new shrub, for Bishop Compton successfully reared a few plants in the uncongenial English soil during 1696 and subsequently. Then the Dutch, with their native talent for making secondhand discoveries, fabricated a legend of trees which had not only flowered, but borne fruit, in the fogs of the Lowlands—adding a rider to this statement by asserting the seed from this source to have been that whence most of the gardens of the East Indies were initiated. It is at least certain that the plant was known to the *savants* of the

West long before its commercial product was familiar to the public.

Probably Coffee as an invigorator is of much older origin than our scanty records on the subject tell us. The Egyptians in the time of the Pharoahs may well have used it, since half their trade lay inland—up the valley of the Nile—to the great Negro cities of its reputed birthplace. The Galla, for instance—a wandering nation of Africa—in their incursions into Abyssinia, being obliged to traverse immense deserts and to travel swiftly, have been accustomed for ages to carry nothing with them to eat but Coffee roasted till it could be pulverised, and then mixed into balls with butter, and put into a leather bag. One of these, the size of a billiard-ball, is said to keep them in strength and spirits during a whole day's fatigue better than either bread or meat.

To Persia—its classic home as a strength-giving draught—we are told to look for the first rise of the art by which the pretty, but hitherto useless, berries were "pulped," roasted, ground and infused, to make that decoction now so dear to Eastern palates. Who endowed The Land of the Lion and Sun with this boon is a moot point, but a Mufti of Aden obtained the secret when on a pilgrimage, and introduced it amongst his followers.

Thence it spread to Turkey,* where, owing

---

* Sir Francis Bacon says: "They have in Turkey a drink called Coffee, made of a berry of the same name, as black as soot, and of probably to the Koranic injunction against its rivals the spirituous liquors, it soon became a popular favourite, and over-rode all opposition from interested pashas and conservative *fakïrs*.*

In our own country, it was at first regarded with great suspicion as a beverage, from the use of which all sorts of terrible evils might be expected to follow. Mr. Edwards, a merchant of Turkey, was perhaps the first to bring the fragrant preparation under British notice. In the year 1650, he imported a Greek youth, named Pasqua Rosee, who was proficient in the art of preparing Coffee; and so greatly did the new drink "take," after the first opposition was over, that in little

---

a strong scent." He was thus probably the initiator of the popular fallacy that Coffee is made from "berries." Latham's edition of "Tod's Johnson's Dictionary" says, that "Coffee is an infusion of the berries." It is no more an infusion of berries than it is of leaves —the "beans" used are of course *seeds*.

* "Coffee comes to us laden with the fragrance of Oriental bazaars and the romance of the 'Arabian Nights.' Its early history as an economic product is involved in considerable obscurity, the absence of historical fact being compensated for by an unusual profusion of conjectural statements, and by purely mythical stories. Throwing legend aside, the use of Coffee seems to have been introduced from Ethiopia into Persia about the year 875 A.D., and into Arabia from the latter country at the beginning of the fourteenth century. Notwithstanding that its use as a beverage was prohibited by the Koran, it spread rapidly through the Mohammedan nation, and it was publicly sold in Constantinople in 1554. It easily found its way from the Levant to Venice, where Coffee-houses were established as early as 1615. A Jew named Jacob opened the first Coffee-house in England, selling it as a common beverage at Baliol College, Oxford, in the year when the Long Parliament met."—*American Paper.*

more than a year, it is said, there were as many Coffee-houses in London as in Constantinople. However this may be, the public seem to have approved of Rosee's speciality. An old advertisement on the subject says the Coffee drink " much quickens the spirits and makes the heart lightsome. It suppresseth fumes exceedingly, and therefore is good against the headache, and will very much stop any defluxion of rheums that distil from the head upon the stomac, and so prevent consumptions and the cough of the lungs. It is excellent to prevent and cure the gout, dropsy, and scurvy. It is known to be better than any other drink for people in years. It is most excellent remedy against the spleen, hypochondriac winds, and the like. It will prevent drowsiness, and make one fit for business if one have occasion to watch; and therefore you are not to drink it after supper unless you intend to be wakeful. It is observed in Turkey, where it is very generally drunk, that they are not troubled with many maladies, or scurvy, and their skins are exceeding clear and white." If at the present time we are hardly able fully to endorse every word of the enthusiastic Greek in praise of his favourite beverage, we can yet feel there can be no doubt he would be gratified could he see the proportions the " trade " has assumed, or know the millions of pounds of British capital invested in the preparation of the article of which he was practically the earliest English champion.

The first Coffee grown in America was, no doubt, introduced into Surinam by the Dutch in 1718. The Governor of Cayenne—De la Motte-Aigron—having been at Surinam, obtained some plants in secret and multiplied them in 1725.

The Coffee plant was introduced into Martinique by De Clieu, a naval officer, in 1720. Thence it was introduced into the other French islands—into Guadaloupe, for instance. In 1730 Sir Nicholas Lawes first grew it in Jamaica. Du Fougerais Grenier introduced Mocha Coffee into Bourbon in 1717. It is known how the cultivation of this shrub has been extended to Java, Ceylon, the West Indies, and Brazil. Nothing prevents it from spreading in all tropical countries, especially as the Coffee plant thrives on sloping ground, and in poor soils where other crops cannot flourish. It corresponds in tropical agriculture with the vine in Europe, and tea in the far East.

Passing on from the commercial to the natural history of the Coffee plant, we will take a brief look at its distribution, species, and habits. The three chief varieties of the plant are easily recognizable to those who have had much to do with Coffee. The Mocha bush, growing on the hot, sandy terraces of the Red Sea littoral, is sparse of leaves and somewhat gaunt and stunted in appearance, as beseems a thing of the desert. Looking at the signs of its condensed vitality, it appears easy to understand the aromatic pungency of its dwarfed berries, which have never been equalled by any achievement of scientific cultivation. Liberian Coffee, on the other hand, is freer of growth, as is natural to a plant whose habitat is among the alluvial flats of low altitudes; the leaves are broad and abundant, the berries big and somewhat coarse: they pay the planter who sells by gross weight better than the finer product, but make a poor beverage. The third, or so-called Arabian Coffee, is the plant most generally cultivated, and holds an intermediate place between the former, both in point of growth and intrinsic value of its yield.

A new Coffee, that may be of importance in the future, called "Maragogipe," has lately been discovered in Brazil, and a Commission was formed to investigate the qualities of the Coffee and also of the plant, and they decided entirely in its favour. Not only does it produce a greater crop, but the Coffee berry is much larger, and possesses a very silky-looking smooth surface, with high quality flavour. It stands well on the high lands, and the first planters who have adopted it in Brazil are so delighted with the results that they are cutting down their splendid Coffee trees of the older kind of Coffee and planting this new "Maragogipe" variety. A gentleman who has just returned from visiting many of the higher estates in Brazil found the planters speaking in the highest terms of this new species of Coffee. Von Glehn, of London, writes :—"The Maragogipe Coffee tree which I have seen growing in Brazil, on the plantations of Mr. Francisco Clemente Pinto, has a much larger leaf than the ordinary Arabian tree. It grows with extraordinary vigour, and trees three to four years old were already eight to ten feet high, and full of fruit. The tree seems to come into full bearing much sooner than the ordinary sort, and the bean is very much larger. Altogether the weight of Coffee per acre must be very much more when the land is planted with Maragogipe than with the ordinary Coffee tree."

Lately the Minister of Agriculture dispatched the following official note to the President of the Province, in relation to the propagation of the new species of plant there discovered :—"The species of Coffee called 'Maragogipe,' which, according to information in this Department of State, was discovered in your Province by Crisogno José Fernandes, has found great favour among the planters of Rio de Janeiro, and the merchants who have examined it in this market, and in various countries of Europe, all agreeing that in size of berry, aroma, and taste it is one of the species most recommendable. With a purpose, therefore, of propagating its cultivation, your Excellency is hereby authorized to acquire, on account of this Department, and to remit 500 kilogrammes of this fruit, in a condition suitable for the plantation. Also, I recommend that your Excellency order the extension of the cultivation existing there to be verified, and the results which it has produced, as well as under what conditions can be obtained the greatest quantity of seeds, having in consideration the vigour of the plant, the time of harvest, the price, and the guarantees of origin and quality."

To botanists, *Coffea Arabica* is a species coming under the class *Pentandria Monogynia* of Linnæus, and the family *Rubiaceæ*, though by some it is placed among the *Cinchonaceæ*, with a good show of reason; but this botanical quibble matters little. It is, in cultivation, a shrub of close and systematic growth. Where allowed to follow its own natural instincts, in uncleared jungle or old and forsaken plantations, it grows to a height of fourteen to eighteen feet, and is then a tall, slight bush, with a straight stem free of branches for the greater part of its height; and an abundance of fine, fibrous roots underground, with a deep-penetrating and all-important "tap root," whose welfare is bound up with that of the plant. Dwarfed by the pruning-knife of the cultivator, it rarely exceeds an elevation of six feet in light sandy soils, and nine feet in the very richest. The latter is an unusual height, and as a matter of experience, I have noticed, when riding through the best-managed estates of Lower India, that the topmost twigs of the plants have rarely been higher than my knees when bestriding a hill pony, which would be something less than five feet from the ground. If allowed to grow higher than this, the difficulties of efficient cultivation and picking are enhanced.

The branches of the plant are placed in pairs on opposite sides of the stem, each pair having its longitudinal axis at right angles to the next. In shape the leaves are similar to those of the Portuguese laurel, smooth and polished on the upper surface, pale red-green when just unfolded, and dark olive when older. This contrast of colour is pleasing and striking when the plants are making new growths. In Sumatra and elsewhere, we read, these tender young leaves are used as a common beverage amongst the natives, who attribute to them many advantages. They "possess slightly tonic and stimulating qualities," without the exciting effects of the decoction from the roasted bean. Though naturally far cheaper as a drink than the preparation of berries, and less marked in its effects on the nervous system, it probably requires an educated taste to be appreciated; and neither the efforts of Dr. Gardner, who patented and exhibited a process in the Great Exhibition of 1851 for the preparation of *Coffee-tea*, nor several other efforts in the same direction, have, as yet, served to bring the drink into popular use. Occasionally, young and soft shoots and leaves are used by the Singhalese to flavour their curries, but these two uses sum up the purposes to which this portion of the plant can be applied.

From the axil of each pair of leaves, when the

plants are in full vigour, spring clusters of twelve to sixteen flower-buds, these opening at the blossoming season with great rapidity. The planter goes over his young estate one morning, probably, in March, and sees the long arrays of healthy shrubs, watched and tended with so much care, heavy with green clustering buds full of promise for a bumper crop, and he rises a morning or two afterwards to behold the whole extent of hill and valley under cultivation a wide-spreading expanse of snow-white blossom, almost hiding the dark green carpet of foliage, and reminding him of hoar frosts in his own far away country, or of its hawthorn hedges in May. The scent from this mass of bloom is very powerful. My own coolies have frequently asked for extra remuneration when carrying letters, or otherwise passing through estates in the full flush of blossoming, declaring such duty frequently gave them attacks of fever. However this may be, the Coffee flower, in colour, odour, and form, is pleasant enough to English senses—a great favourite with the natives for decking their images of Buddha, &c. Botanically it is said to be " axillary, sessile, calyx monopetalous, funnel-shaped, and cut at the limb into fine, reflexed, lanceolate segments."

There are generally two—sometimes three—relays of blossom before all the buds have arrived at maturity (which is, no doubt, owing to the number of buds in each cluster preventing their all coming out together), but the principal one is generally the first which comes out in March. After a day or two, the flowers gradually turn brown, and fade away; the slower and more gradual this process is, the better. Rainfall, while the blossoms are out, is much to be deprecated; but once the latter has set, a good shower will be beneficial rather than otherwise. This will wash off the withered petals, leaving exposed to view the numerous pistils, or fruit germs, upon which all depends. These should have fresh, whitish tips, to indicate a healthy appearance; and when this is the case, the blossoms are said to have "set well," and a crop may be looked for proportionate to the abundance of the blossom. Sometimes, however, an ominous little black speck is discernible in the centre of the pistil; and where this is the case, fructification will not follow. This is most commonly the result of inopportune rain while the flowers are out; or it may follow a prolonged season of drought, and be due to a weakly condition of the plant.

Beautiful while they last, and delighting the planter's eye with their likeness to the flowers of the English hedgerows in spring time, or filling him with pleasant thoughts of future profits, accordingly as sentiment or practicability dominate in his mind, their life is yet short, and in three or four days the beauty of the plantation is gone, and the petals lie yellow and withered on the ground.

From the short stalks whence they have fallen

rise groups of berries, at first yellow and hard to the touch, lying in the hollows of the leaves. As they ripen under the influence of a meridian sun, their colour deepens—not regularly, but by crimson and scarlet shades and tints which spread over the skin until about October its surface is covered, and the "cherry" (for so it is now called by a happy comparison with the familiar fruit) has mellowed to a deep glossy purple-black, with a smooth and bloomless cuticle.

Laborie, whose works are of undiminished value though amongst the oldest on the planter's shelves, waxes eloquent over the charms of the Coffee bush in its various stages of growth. "In both states, of flower and fruit, nature is nowhere more profuse and beautiful in the variety of its colours and forms," he writes, and we feel much sympathy with his enthusiasm. At this period the cherry is picked, some little experience being required to know just the right time, which is when the fruit feels quite soft to the touch, and a few of the ripest are already falling to the ground. Different sides of a bush will be ready on different days, and different aspects may be as much as a week apart in ripening. This is a boon to the planter, who has his hands very full at this busiest of all seasons.

The cherry has many and voracious enemies. A few birds wax fat on the sweet pulp at the planter's expense; Sambur deer are not above an occasional raid into the gardens, while jackals and monkies are fond of the ripe fruit.

"Monkey or Jackal Coffee," once highly valued as the choicest form of berry procurable for drinking purposes, is simply the undigested Coffee seeds which have passed unaltered through the intestinal canal of the animal that has stolen them, and have been left about in the jungles. Elliot does not believe in "Jackal Coffee," regarding the name as applicable "to the seeds that have been knocked off the trees, or spilt by the pickers, of green berries that will not ripen, and of stray berries that have dried on the trees." With all due deference to that accomplished writer, we can only point to the well-known facts with which every planter is familiar. Dr. Shortt, in his "Handbook of Planting for Southern India," devotes some space to the consideration of the reasons why such berries make a better beverage than others. We take a central position between these authorities, holding with one that the appreciation of such stercoraceously deposited beans by natives is an undoubted fact, and with the other that they are of little or no superior value to those plucked in an ordinary way from the trees.

To return to the subject of the berries just ripened upon their bushes. We have seen they have many admirers besides the legitimate owner, and this is wholly on account of the sweet pulp Several experiments have been made to utilize this succulent covering, but without much success. The chemistry of waste products has yet an inexhaustible field before it, and our cherry covering is an instance.

As manure, we shall mention it again. It is in this form of moderate value, like any other vegetable refuse, but contains too large a portion of water in the crude state to recommend it highly to the economical planter. Spirit is occasionally distilled from it, but not in India; and abroad, dried and pounded, it has been tried as a substitute for Coffee with but very poor results.

It is, however, with the seed it covers we have most interest. This, in its barest form, cannot fail to be familiar to everyone who has looked into the shops of towns or cities and observed large stores of "Ceylon Plantation," "Mocha," "Native Ceylon," or "Rio" Coffee piled up in heaps and ready for sale. In that condition it is chocolate-colour—roasted; and unroasted, of a greenish-grey tint, varying slightly with the nature and growth of the species. These pale green "beans"—for that is their technical name (derived from the Arabic word *bunn*, an authority tells us, and thus from the same root as the humble cake)—are convex on one surface and flat upon the other. In the centre of the ripe fruit two of them lie close together (smooth surface to smooth surface), each covered first by a very fine and delicate garment, termed "the silvery skin;" nextly, each has a somewhat rougher cartilaginous membrane of smooth, shiny consistency, for this reason called the parchment. Above the latter comes the pulp, "mucilaginous, saccharine, and somewhat glutinous," as an exact author terms it; and, outside again, there is the external skin.

Coffee varies in colour from brown to bluish green. Not only do Coffee seeds vary in colour, but also in size. The following table will give an idea of the size of the berries, and also of the comparative value of Coffee from different localities:—

	No. of Seeds in a Unit Measure holding 50 Grams of Water (about 2½ ozs.)	Per Cwt. £ s.
Fine brown Java	187	8 0
Fine Mysore	198	6 10
Fine Neilgherry	203	4 13
Costa Rica	203	3 10
Good ordinary Guatemala ..	207	2 16
Good La Guayra	210	3 10
Good average Santos ...	213	2 14
*Fine long berry Mocha ...	217	6 10
*Good ordinary Java ...	223	3 0
Fine Ceylon Plantation ...	225	4 12
*Good average Rio	236	2 12
Medium Plantation (Ceylon)	238	3 18
*Manilla	248	2 12
*Ordinary Mocha	270	5 0
*West African	313	2 0

Those sorts which are marked with an asterisk are irregular in size and colour, and have the appearance of being carelessly prepared; and the reason why Rio, Manilla, and West African fetch the least money seems obvious enough.

The high prices of the Mochas lead one to think that there is something in a name, but the light colour of the seeds indicates probably not only a very complete ripeness when gathered, but considerable age as well; and be it remembered that *Coffee improves with age*, and will continue to improve for fifteen or twenty years. The brown Java, priced at 160*s*., has not only very fine seeds, but it has been six or seven years in the island. If Coffee be kept in a dry place it matures and improves. It loses water, gets lighter, and when roasted developes more aroma. The fact that Coffee can be stored in bulk for household use, and continues to improve with age, should recommend it to the careful housewife. "C'est l'âge qui fait le bon Café," says the writer of the monograph, "Le Brésil à l'Exposition Internationale d'Amsterdam."

In preparing Coffee after it is plucked from the trees, the pulp is removed by water and fermentation, and the *parchment* subsequently shred from the *beans* by passing them between carefully-adjusted rollers and winnowing. It is then ready for sale and transport, and this is all the work of preparation that falls to the planter's hands.

"To dream of drinking Coffee," says De Candolle, "is a favourable omen, betokening riches and honours." To dream of planting it, and to follow up the vision practically, may lead to a like result if skill and caution guide affairs and characterise the planter's operations.

CHAPTER II.

SOIL AND CLIMATE.

As a general rule, it is said, the best zone of latitude for Coffee is 150° on each side of the equator, of altitude from 3,000 to 4,500 feet. The deeper, freer, and richer the soil is the better. It should be specially tested for phosphoric acid and potash. The latter will be in abundance when a large forest has been felled, but burned grass land must be very good to grow Coffee.

Soil and climate are subjects of primitive importance if our garden is to succeed and our crops to be bumper ones.

Looking at soil from an annalist's point of view, says Pogson, we find it consists of an *organic* part, which placed in the fire will burn away, and an *inorganic* or mineral part, which will not. The constitution of the first is well known. It is formed by remains of animals, insects, minute visible and invisible organisms of various kinds, from the dung of animals, birds, caterpillars, and worms, and from the roots, stems, and leaves of decayed vegetables. The inorganic part consists of sand, clay, lime, magnesia, oxides of iron, oxides of maganese, potash, soda, sulphuric acid, phosphoric acid, carbonic acid. The preponderance of one or more of the natural divisions makes the soil productive or unproductive, while certain plants make special calls upon one or more substances, and consequently such must be present and available in a soil that is to suit them.

Officially, five kinds of soil are recognized in India, but in truth there are a greater variety than in any other country in the world except China.

A rich soil generally contains five per-cent., or one twentieth, of its weight of organic matter in combination with other fertilizing substances. As for the best ground for Coffee in particular, it may be noted that our chief authorities differ in their views; but as a broad principle the best soil is the *richest*, no matter what its colour, or whether it be the volcanic mould of Java, the rich red earth of Brazil, the deep valley silt of Arabia, or the Ceylon jungle mould.

Sabonadière's description of a good soil's exterior character is as good as any we have read. "We come to the conclusion," he says, "that a dark chocolate-coloured soil mixed with small stones, under ledges of rock, and bestrewn with boulders, is most suitable for the trees." In this he will be found to have given a very accurate description of much of the best ground in Ceylon and Southern India. It is plain, however, that he has only given the superficial and casual characteristics of a suitable earth, since many causes may produce the dark colour he admires, and the fact that land is bestrewn with small fragments of rocks and scattered boulders can have only a remote influence on the yield of fruit.

In general, a fair idea of the nature of any soil can be obtained by a study of the jungle that grows upon it. Scattered "sholas," or clumps of trees interspersed with expanses of waving lemon grass and such like—picturesque as it may be— will never do for the shrub, since they show a shallow soil on layers of rock. Rather we must seek to find thick, heavy jungle, close grown, with soft-wooded trees, such as the sacred fig, creepers, tree-ferns, and giant lichens. Where these abound and grow luxuriantly, the earth below them is certain to be richly loaded with decayed vegetation, and thus fulfils one requirement of the planter. Parasitic plants—and especially orchids, I have noticed (though their connection with the soil is but secondhand)—seem to indicate and thrive best on the richest ground. The presence of trees of large and free growth, running up straight to the sky and, as it were, racing for precedence, points to a good depth of mould under their roots.

Plants in general, and Coffee in particular, require a soil free from stagnant water, sufficiently friable to be open to the passage of air for admitting of "respiration," and possessing a sufficiency of those constituents which are essential to the growth and nourishment of the vegetable.

Coffee, as previously noted, is tap-rooted, and it is essential to its proper well-being that this root may penetrate down into the body of the earth, where should lie those reservoirs of moisture and manure that must be looked to for nourishment and support during trying times of drought and sunshine. This points to the necessity of a deep and penetrable soil. Where mould, no matter how good, is shallow, and rests on hard clay or "slab" rock at small depth, planting is useless; an admixture of gravel, however—or, more properly speaking, the hill shale so common in Coffee districts—is not a bar to success if the surrounding circumstances are favourable. Ground broken up for the first time under the shade of primeval forest, it will commonly happen, however, possesses such a depth of mould that practically the subsoil is non-existent. In my own region of Southern India much of our Coffee was on four and six feet of rich black earth that crumbled to the touch, being both "warm" and "free" in texture. This, of course, in the more favoured hollows of the valleys, and such a depth is not to be looked for everywhere.

It will be as well for the young planter to remember that an estate may have everything to commend it to the external view, and fulfil to a nicety all the conditions he has been taught to seek, and yet disappoint when the crucial test of crop times comes. On some land the plants thrive amazingly for a time, vigorous in growth and glossy in foliage. Such promise is deceptive, and the bushes never achieve anything beyond a plentiful harvest of leaves. Other districts, again, seeming to invite cultivation, rear Coffee entertaining a curious liability to suffer attacks from various foes and diseases.

The secret of these variations no one quite understands. They form a still vexed question, upon which there are probably as many opinions as planters. Every country—and not only every country, but every district—has its peculiarities and traditions. These can hardly be understood except by personal inspection. Planters, as a rule, scorn laboratory tests, preferring to judge by rule of thumb in their selection of garden sites. They are usually right, and the beginner is lucky who can get an old hand in the district to ride over and give him a friendly opinion on the capabilities of his proposed location!

After all is said, the Coffee plant is a hardy shrub; and though the best soils for it can be only recognized by experience, the fact that it is spread over all parts of the world, and is fruitful on the sandy terraces of the Arabian littoral or the moist, alluvial flats of Gambia, tends towards showing it has a wide range of tastes.

The following opinions of writers on the question of soil will be read with interest, and are instructive in marking the uniformity of judgment amongst them.

Sabonadière says, in "The Coffee Planter of Ceylon:"

"The most suitable soil for the Coffee bush is that which grows soft timber. The hard 'doon' wood (useful, however, for shingles and beams) is usually found on high quartzy ridges, which both the nature of the soil and exposure to winds render unsuitable. The best land for Coffee is a dark chocolate-coloured soil, mixed with small stones and overspread here and there with boulders of granite. . . . . Those estates where slab rock, gravel, or clay prevail are worked at a questionably remunerative return, and must ere long be abandoned as not paying for their cultivation."

In *Mr. Hull's* opinion ("Coffee Planting in Southern India"):—

"When the soil is dark in colour, loose, and full of roots, it is rich in organic matter, and therefore good for Coffee, which is a hardy plant not on the whole difficult to please in this matter. . . . . The best criterion as to the quality of the soil is the luxuriousness or otherwise of the vegetation it produces in its original state. For instance, in forests which, in addition to a large growth of timber, have a dense close underwood and abound in mosses and ferns, if may safely be concluded the soil is good."

An experienced writer in *Balfour's* excellent "Cyclopædia of India" says:—

"In Ceylon the best soil is a deep chocolate colour, friable and abounding with blocks and small pieces of stone.

Such patches of land are generally found at the bottom of the escarpments of the hills or in elevated valleys, and rarely on the slopes. Quartoze land must be carefully avoided, and clay is equally bad. A good surface soil should have at least two feet of depth, as the Coffee tree has a long tap root."

Mr. P. L. Simmonds remarks in his "Tropical Agriculture:"

"Coffee trees flourish in hilly districts where the subsoil is gravelly, for the roots will strike down and obtain nourishment so as to keep the plant alive and fruitful for thirty years. Trees planted in a light soil, and in a dry and elevated spot, produce smaller berries, which have a better flavour than those grown in rich, flat, and moist soils. The weight of produce yielded by the latter is, however, double that obtained from the former; and, as the difference in price between the two is by no means adequate to cover this deficiency of weight, the interest of the planter naturally leads him to the production of the largest but least excellent kind."

A writer on American Coffee tells us :—

"The best crops that I have seen have been on a rich black loam, too rocky to be worked with the plough, and on the slopes of ravines. It is said that the plant dies out in a few years on clay soil. But the Liberian plant is said to flourish on such soil. I attribute the better condition of the plants on sloping ground to the fact of their being more shaded. It is generally held that the Coffee will not flourish on wet ground, though the best plants I ever saw [as far as leaves went?] were within a few feet of an unfailing stream."

And "An Old Planter" thinks we should look to the subsoil:

"A rich chocolate is my favourite, and I have generally seen the best estates where that was the body of the soil.

But a deep black is also good—sometimes, indeed, very fine. And there are other kinds not to be despised. A free, friable kind of soil is generally a very desirable first condition, whatever be the colour. But it should not be sandy, clayey or ferruginous. If well studded with large boulders so much the better. These keep the soil together, as well as improve it by the process of their decay. Avoid land where there is much slab-rock cropping out on the surface, however. The soil is seldom deep upon such rock, and it gradually slides away: while even before it slips, the roots of the Coffee trees coming in contact with the hidden rock cause the tree to wither and die when in its very prime."

The matter of climate is at least as important as the previous one, and can be approached with more confidence of accuracy. That also of *aspect* is worth consideration. Coffee of one sort or another will grow and thrive more or less from the sea level to 6,000 feet of elevation.

In Ceylon the result of much experience and innumerable failures from too much humidity, or an excess of dryness in the atmosphere, has led to the conclusion that a height of 3,000 feet, with a divergence of 500 feet higher or lower, is the best elevation that can be chosen.

The highest estate of Travancore is in Velavengodu district, at an elevation of 3,900 feet; but there are only two estates there, which comprise unitedly 395 acres, and the outturn of which has been 412 lbs. per acre of mature plants. The lowest estate is in Neduvengaud, altitude above the sea about 400 feet; and on this 154 lbs. per acre were gathered. The average produce for all plantations was about 276 lbs. per acre of full-grown plants. Where the cost of cultivation is greatest the out-turn also is greatest. In the two highest estates mentioned the cost of cultivation was said to be Rs. 111 per acre.

It must be borne in mind, while considering this subject, that Coffee requires—(1) a suitable soil, (2) a temperate climate within the tropics, (3) a range of heat between 60° and 80° Fahrenheit, and (4) a rainfall of not less than 80 inches, falling chiefly in the monsoon or planting season, but never withheld for many weeks at a spell.

Ceylon is, as a rule, more humid than India. It is encircled on every side by the sea, and hence the collection of clouds and consequent rainfall is in excess of that of India, where the rain comes in certain consecutive wet months, followed by half-a-year of cloudless skies and parching winds. As a consequence, it may be roundly stated that 3,000 feet in that island of palms and spices will be equivalent to 4,000 feet in India, since the heat and dryness of the latter must be met by ascending to greater and cooler elevations.

This general principle suffers modification from such causes as aspect, local peculiarities of climate, abundance of forest shade, and special cultivation. For instance, many native gardens around Colombo growing *Coffee Arabica* are at the sea level, but then they are overshadowed by thickets of foliage, abundantly manured, and carefully watered in the hot weather. Some European estates on the Neilgherries, in Madras, on the other hand, are 6,000 feet above the plain, and in that delightful region there seems no limit to the available area, stopping short only at the line of frosts.

In Ceylon an eastern aspect is considered desirable. In Southern India Elliot argues strongly in favour of a northern slope, since it loses less of its moisture, stored during the monsoon, than the opposite slope, exposed to the vertical rays of a sun, and preserves a more equal temperature. Eastern and western slopes are more equal in respect to the influence exerted upon them by the sun, and thus advantageous or the contrary according to their exposure to rainfall and wind.

It must be remembered that while the influence of too much heat upon unshaded Coffee is palpable in the gaunt, famished bushes, and their sickly array of yellow leaves, the opposite extreme of an excess of cold and moisture, though equally fatal in its effect upon the actual crop of cherries, is more delusive, and for a long time the bushes growing under such circumstances delight the inexperienced eye by their wealth of verdure.

A garden so placed, high up on a mountain side, where all the water-laden clouds from the sea first strike and go to pieces upon the barrier, discharging their freights of rain and mist, is a disappointing investment. The Coffee is planted and flourishes amazingly. Soon the soil of the garden can hardly be seen anywhere for the rich green carpet of glossy foliage that covers it; but this is all. The crop never comes, or comes very thinly, and will not ripen. This is only natural when we remember that we are here growing a tropical plant under the atmospheric conditions of northern countries.

The golden rule applies to India as well as all other countries, that a happy mean must be hit—temperature about 60° or 80° Fahrenheit, and rainfall 80 inches per year.

Annexed is four years' rainfall of a central district of Ceylon:—

Month.	Inches.	Inches.	Inches.	Inches.
January	3.48	5.89	11.39	14.26
February	7.09	8.25	2.10	8.86
March	5.64	13.95	2.02	6.17
April	9.00	7.38	6.48	3.77
May	5.92	0.55	4.28	4.97
June	0.59	1.38	3.36	1.67
July	6.70	3.18	4.03	2.83
August	3.86	3.75	3.29	5.79
September	7.32	2.48	6.02	1.36
October	4.16	15.50	19.18	11.13
November	11.49	19.85	8.79	18.30
December	9.50	12.25	19.84	15.36
Totals	74.75	94.42	91.41	94.47

Trinidad in the West Indies has only 65 inches in the year; Upper Rajawalla in Dumbara (Ceylon) shows a yearly average of 55.78 inches; Kurunegala, 84.09. Upon Delgolla, another Ceylon estate, nearly 100 inches fall per year. In the Indian jungles, with which I am most familiar, we sometimes had as much as 120 inches in the twelve months.

The total average rainfall in each district of Madras ranges thus:—

District.	Inches.	District.	Inches.
South Canara	143.60	Nellore	36.47
Malabar	114.95	Salem	35.30
Madras	57.96	Trichinopoly	34.94
Chingleput	48.22	Kistna	32.58
South Arcot	44.77	Cuddapah	30.97
Ganjam	44.03	Kurnool	30.01
Tanjore	43.49	Coimbatore	24.81
Vizagapatam	40.65	Bellary	25.77
North Arcot	40.34	Madura	23.73
Godavari	39.28	Tinnevelly	22.85

It is to be noted that the rainfall given above is merely the average for a district, and that it not unfrequently happens that the rainfall in one part of a district varies as widely from that in another part of the same district as it does from that in stations in other districts, if not more so.

If, in spite of any feasible elevation that can be reached, the tropical sun will have its way, and pours down on the baked soil, threatening destruction to all but the deepest rooted vegetation, then we must have recourse to shade-trees, and grow our Coffee in an imitation of its native jungles. In fact, trees are of the first importance to regulate the climate of a country.

Lieut.-Col. Beddome, in his Report to the Famine Commissioners, gives a striking instance of the damage indiscriminate felling of forests works to a district, and we can fully corroborate his remarks, knowing the Mettapolliem gorge well :—

"The clearing away of forests protecting a spring or head of a stream almost always dries it up, and the denudation of the forests protecting the slopes of ravines down which it runs seriously affects it, causing a great rush of water after heavy rain and corresponding diminution at other times. These facts are too patent to require proof, but can be established by most forest officers. To illustrate the ill effects of deforesting steep mountain ravines I could mention nothing more appropriate than the Coonoor ghat ravine, the approach to the Nilgiri from Mettapolliem. I have been up and down this many times nearly every year since 1857, and watched the gradual destruction of the forest, trying hard to stop it, but with what result is very evident, although Government have passed several orders forbidding the clearance of the forests. When I first knew it the ravine was all forest-clad, both sides, and in the heaviest rain there was no very apparent wash of the soil, no land slips or rolling boulders, and the rivulets feeding the river down the centre of the ravine all running tolerably clear. Now the north-east slopes or the slopes above the road have been almost entirely deforested, and it is quite dangerous to go up the ghat during very heavy rain, which often occurs in October, November, and the beginning of December, and sometimes in May. Boulders of rock of various sizes, from several cwts. to 100 tons, come rolling down, rendering the old and new ghats impassable and destroying the bridges, and the soil in many places pours over the road like lava, and the water in the streams is of the consistency of cream. Most of this deforested land has been planted with Coffee, and many people would argue with advantage to the State; but the forest officer says steep mountain slopes like this must be protected from denudation for Coffee, as it is utterly impossible that the soil can last very long. The forest has now been replaced by Coffee, and in the future Coffee will be replaced by a rocky barren mountain slope with no trees or cultivation of any sort, and the State will then say how improvident our ancestors were. Tree-planting will then be too expensive."

This, however, is a subject that will be glanced at subsequently.

Insect life is a danger to Coffee that is considerably influenced by climate. An excess of wet encourages the "black bug," a deadly form of blight, and a great range of temperature from high to low produces a million foes to the planter in the form of insect life or an overflow of rank weeds.

There is one other thing that must not be overlooked in forming a plantation, and that is the force and nature of the winds beating upon the ground. It is almost impossible to say anything upon this subject except that the young planter will do well to get his plants as much sheltered as possible by forests, by ranges of hills, or by belts of woodland left standing when the jungle is felled, and more especially when the wind is one of much the same character—either a very hot blast or a very wet one. The former singes vegetation, and often at the time when plants are fruiting and in need of all available strength, the latter beats the bushes to ribbons, snaps their tender rootlets as they are formed, and does unlimited damage to an exposed site by hurtling the seasonal rains against it, thus washing into the ravines with each muddy torrent all its best soil. The aspect of the jungle trees will often indicate the nature of the winds that beat upon them. A tempest-swept soil usually presents a hardened and washed-out appearance which a little experience will enable one to detect.

The planter must see to the sheltering of his Coffee as best he can in this respect, and should remember that the rules which suit his next door neighbour will by no means of a necessity apply to him.

We may quote *Elliot* on this subject. Speaking of the Indian monsoons, he says:—

"These south-west winds are, however, only fatally injurious on the first barrier of hills they strike. Further inland their force is greatly modified, and to such an extent that little injury results from them. For instance, along the whole of the westerly frontier range of the Mysore tableland Coffee can hardly be grown at all in face of the south-west monsoon, and eastern aspects are therefore the best; while five miles further inland an eastern aspect, from the climate being so much drier and hotter, is most to be avoided, and a western aspect may be considered rather favourable than otherwise."

To sum up: a perusal of the foregoing suggestions should give the beginner, no matter what part of the world he may be in, some idea of those adverse circumstances to avoid in forming his garden, modified only perhaps by the species of Coffee he cultivates; but as Coffee Arabica is almost invariably the plant grown by English, this latter clause is not of much importance.

He must not locate himself in a shadeless torrid zone, swept by parching winds, or the first hot spell after the trees have come to maturity will wither their leaves and his hopes at the same time. If he goes high up the mountains amongst the drifting clouds, he will get into a climate wetter and even colder than the English, and will possess in the fulness of time a garden admirably suited for producing the ingredients of Coffee-leaf tea, but little else. He may be fond of a sea view, but must remember that sea winds are laden with over much moisture, while those from the land are usually deficient in that very respect. To strike the happy mean between extreme adverse points, and to modify nature where he cannot control her, is half the planter's art.

CHAPTER III.

LABOUR AND LABOURERS.

It is a stern fact, unfortunately impossible to ignore, that to grow Coffee we must employ labour, and to a large extent.

Natives of most warm countries—and certainly of Lower India—are physically inferior to the working classes of the invigorating north. Doctors tell us the blood of dark races is thinner—there are fewer red corpuscules in a given quantity than with European. For this, as for other reasons, native vital energy is lower and their powers less than in our own and other white races.

Mr. Monier Williams' recent volume, " Modern India," should be in the hands of every Coffee planter. He tells us, in a single paragraph, the history and characteristics of the chief races of labourers with whom the Indian planter comes in contact:

" Southern India, not including Aryan Orissa, is peopled first by the great Dravidian races (so called from Dravida, the name given by the Sanskrit speakers to the southern part of the Peninsula), whose immigrations into India in successive waves from some part of Central Asia immediately preceded those of the Aryans. These Dravidians are of course quite distinct from the Aryans; their skin is generally much darker, and the languages they speak belong to what is called the South

Turanian family. They may be separated into four distinct peoples, according to their four principal languages—Telugu, Canarese, Tamil, and Malayalam. Secondly, by the wild aboriginal races, some of them Negroid, and as dark in complexion as Africans, and others of a type similar to the savages of Australia. They are now usually called Kolarians. Their irruptions preceded the advent of the Dravidians, and they are still found in the hills and other outlying localities. Of the Dravidians the Telugu and Tamil speakers are by far the majority, each numbering fifteen or sixteen millions. The Tamil race, who occupy the extreme south from Madras to Cape Comorin, are active, hard-working, industrious, and independent. Their difficult and highly accentuated language reflects their character, and possesses quite a distinct literature of its own. The Telugu people, inhabiting the Northern Circars and the Nizam's territory, are also remarkable for their industry, and their soft language, abounding in vowels, is the Italian of the East. The Canarese of Mysore resemble the Telugu race in language and character, just as the Malayalams of the Malabar coast resemble the Tamils. I noticed that the seafaring Tamils of the southern coast near Ramnad, Ramesvaram, and Tuticorin are much more able-bodied and athletic than ordinary Hindoos. Numbers of them migrate to Ceylon, and at least half-a-million form a permanent part of the population of that island. They are to be found in all the Coffee plantations, and work much harder than the Singhalese. Indeed, all the races of South India seem to me to show readiness and aptitude for any work they are required to do, and great patience, endurance, and perseverance in the discharge of the most irksome duties. The lower classes may be seen everywhere earning their bread by the veritable sweat of their brow, and submitting without a murmur to a life of drudgery and privation. But they are not, as a rule, physically strong, and their moral character, like their bodily constitution, exhibits little stamina."

Whatever the descent of the coolies employed (and districts often vary greatly in this respect), the estate work is usually done by labourers who reside upon it, and take weekly wages from the owners or their representatives. This is especially the case in new districts surrounded by wild country. In older neighbourhoods there may be populous villages hard by whence labour can be drawn day by day; and occasionally the work, or portions of it, are put out to contractors.

In the first case, the procedure is somewhat as follows: The planter goes to the lowlands and puts himself in communication with half-a-dozen "Maistries," "Kanganies," or head men, to whom he communicates his needs in the way of labour. They assure him they can obtain a good and sufficient supply, and are forthwith provided with advances (a signed and witnessed agreement having been made with them)—*i.e.*, Rs. 5, or so—for each man they agree to find. This money is supposed to pass into the coolie's hands, and act as an inducement for him to leave home, or as something to support the family while he is away.

At the stipulated time the Maistries appear in the jungle, each at the head of his gang of coolies, all heavily loaded with earthen "chatties" or cooking pans, native shawls, supplies of dried fish, curry stuffs, &c.; and "salaaming" to the European, they settle down, building themselves "lines" or huts, if there are none ready, and working off those advances entered (on the first occasion when they are all mustered) against their names in the estate books.

This is the simplest way in which labour is imported. When it comes from remote districts, or even across the sea (Malay labour has been tried in Northern India), the expense, as will readily be understood, is greatly increased.

Lieut.-Col. Edward Money says on this subject, in his admirable "Cultivation and Manufacture of Tea:"*

"Each coolie imported costs Rs. 30 and upwards (it used to be much more) ere he arrives on the garden and does any work. After arrival he has to be housed; to be cared for and physicked when sick; to be paid when ill as when working; to have work found for him, or paid to sit idle when there is no work; and, in addition to all this, every death, every desertion, is a loss to the garden of the whole sum expended in bringing the man or woman. Contrast this with the advantages of local labour. In many cases no expense for buildings is necessary, as the labourers come daily to work from adjacent villages, and in such cases no expense is entailed by sick men, for these simply remain at home. There is no loss by death or desertions. When no work is required on the garden, labour is simply not employed. All this makes local labour, even where the rate of wages is high, very much cheaper than imported."

Contract labour again, where it is possible, has many and obvious advantages. The manager of the estate is freed from the petty and harassing worries resulting from personal care of workmen. Yet, if this arrangement of giving jungle-felling,

---

* Published by Messrs. W. B. Whittingham and Co., 91, Gracechurch Street, E.C.

building, road-opening, or what not, into a contractor's hands has advantages and looks feasible, it has its drawbacks.

The troubles which the planter escapes of uncertain labour supply, unpropitious weather, and all similar difficulties, weigh equally upon the responsible native to whom he transfers them. That person may commence his task, proceed a certain way with it, and then become a fraudulent absentee, or his funds may really give out, or he may not finish the allotted task within the prescribed time—any of which is very painful. Planters—and especially those whose practical experience is limited—advise the taking of sureties and bonds when a contract is formed for estate work. The chief objection to this is that few natives are in a position to give any adequate forfeit money; and those who might, usually will not!

My experience leads me to believe, work the men really understand, and earn their usual living from, will generally be done well and honourably by them. I have, for instance, employed gangs of Tamils as sawyers, and others as fellers of forest. They brought their own tools; built their own huts, according to fancy; had abundance of the food they were accustomed to, and received far the largest portion of their money on finishing and leaving. A mutually satisfactory result to both sides was the usual result. But, on the other hand, when a Hindoo, more distinguished for his push than business integrity, brought up a band of bazaar loafers and station hangers-on for my early building operations, the result was eminently unpleasant all round.

The coolies of certain districts—or special villages, it may be—will be adepts at peculiar operations; and in such they may generally be employed for contract work, under the most creditable and best-known master who offers his services. Of course sureties may be taken, by all means, when they can be had; but in India, at least, the necessary legal formalities are tedious and elaborate. One thing is certain, that with the natives of all lands—but with none more so than the simple, yet keen, natives of the Empire—a straightforward bearing, and an honest interest in their welfare, is one of the readiest roads to success and satisfaction. The coolie gauges his master's mind and weaknesses with a woman's shrewdness. It is a peculiarity of his race to be what the ungracious would term a sycophant; yet he appreciates kindness, and will repay encouragement and consideration with fidelity and zeal.

When the young planter has got his men together —twenty, perhaps, with their allowance of women and children, for the first two hundred acres he opens, and more in proportion—then comes the careful and skilful working of them, his aims being: (1) To get as much work out of them as he reasonably can without (2) being unduly harsh, for in that case they would bolt, his estate would get a bad name, and he would be left entirely without labour.

When the first morning for work comes—and the mornings in the jungle are decidedly raw and cold, with usually a thin, drizzling mist or damp fog hanging about until the sun is up—the planter turns out about 5 a.m., and, after sounding the muster-call on his great bell or gong, makes a hasty toilet and partakes of the invigorating hot Coffee and toast which his "cook boy" has prepared. Then, as soon as the coolies, all swaddled up to their chins in blankets, have sauntered up to the open ground by his hut, he takes his memorandum-book and goes down to divide them according to the work to be done. Twenty men, perhaps, under one maistry, are sent with axes and crowbars to cut and move the logs from the line of a new road; ten or twelve more to weed the "nursery;" so many women and children, under two or three overseers (they always want a lot of looking after), take baskets and hoes and depart to weed the Coffee land already planted; some are sent to fetch grass, some to building, and so on. As each party goes down to the store to get the necessary tools, the assistant has to see that each one takes the right thing and only the right thing, and the building is full of coolies pushing, fighting, and quarrelling, some taking the wrong implements, and some none at all, in spite of vigorous endeavours to get affairs straight. Even when all the natives present at muster have been told off and started with their tools, the day's troubles are only beginning; for no sooner are they clear of the settlement, and winding along the narrow jungle paths, than they make all sorts of attempts to escape and get back to their huts, hoping, by being present at the morning muster and again at evening roll-call, that their absence during the day will not have been noticed, and so they may get pay for doing no work.

Then, when the constant supervision of the day's work is over, comes the evening roll-call, and at the end of the week roll-call and pay-muster in one. Perhaps I may be permitted to quote here a suggestive sketch of a Saturday evening muster, showing how coolies are paid off at the end of the week on Indian and Ceylon estates:

"The first pay-day in the jungle is always a difficult one for the new arrival, especially when he has to be his own paymaster to the forces, his cashier and clerk all rolled in one. The coinage is strange to him, and he is sure to get more or less mixed up in his pice, annas, and rupees, unless he has a head better fitted for a mercantile desk at home than the backwoods. Most of those who try Coffee planting have souls above mathematics, and to them their first experience of paying a horde of coolies (who, like all natives, dote on litigation) will be long remembered as a *dies iræ*. Still it is a thing which has to be done, however unpleasant; but I feel for King James of blessed memory, who naïvely remarked when receiving a petition to pay his Scotch bills, 'Of all petitions this is the one which his Majesty liketh least.'

"Unfortunately for me, the next day after R——'s flight to the lowlands was Saturday, and all day long I was practising rapid reduction of rupees to the smallest coin of the Empire, while striving to draw some consolation from the fact that the estate would have nothing to do with cowery shells, 5,120 of which go to the rupee. The thought of giving or receiving such small change of that sort would be distraction—four pice, or cash, to the anna being quite as much as I could stand with equanimity.

"The day, like its predecessors, was miserably cold and dull, and, fearful of being overtaken by darkness before getting through the paying, the estate bell was rung an hour earlier than usual to recall the coolies to the mustering ground. They came trooping in from all parts in strong force, and apparently with considerable interest, to see what was going to take place. When they were all mustered the crowd was thicker and denser than I had ever seen it before, everybody having turned out, even to the lame and sick who were too ill to go to work.

"When I entered the great circle of nearly two hundred men, women, and children, looking as solemn as might be, with the fateful day-book in one hand and a huge bag of copper and silver coins in the other, having the half-caste clerk at my elbow to interpret, I was conscious that all eyes were upon me, and my smallest motion was being watched in deep silence by the assembled coolies. Determined to get into practice as soon as possible, instead of letting the half-caste call over the names, I determined to do it myself, and, shooting out the bag of money into a glittering heap on the rough wooden table in front of me, plunged at once into the long columns of outlandish names, which filled ten or twelve folio pages of the day-book. Opposite to each name, in our system of book-keeping, there were six rows of columns, one for each day of the week, and in each of these columns there was a whole mark, a half, or a blank, according as the coolie had worked—a whole day, a half-day, or none at all. Beyond these columns was one to record the total number of days worked out of the last six, and then another division to record the pay given out. At the end of the month the columns of each page were added up, both across and up and down, and, if exactly correct, the final reading in the bottom right-hand corner was the same for both. Thus it was impossible to make a mistake of even a pie without being able to discover it; but at the same time, among so many densely packed columns, it was difficult to avoid small errors, which would show up large in the final result, and cause a vast amount of trouble to correct. Thus I had to call each coolie's name first of all, and, if he had been working all day, put him down in the Saturday column with a mark; then add up his total work for the week—say five and a-half days—put this down in the space devoted to it, calculate five and a-half days at five annas a-day (the rate at which we pay our men), put down Rs. 1 11a. 2p. in the pay space, count it out of the heap of coinage at my elbow, give it to the man, and dismiss him.

"This may sound simple enough, but there were many little difficulties to be surmounted. When I began calling the fearful and wonderful Tamil and Canarese names there was a general titter round the circle, and three or four men answered at once, my pronunciation being so shaky that they could not distinguish whose name it was. However, I suppressed the giggling, and having obtained 'silence in the court,' forged slowly ahead, every now and then making some mistake which set the natives smiling, but getting slowly into the way of the pronunciation, and running up the sums and counting out the change like a booking clerk. Often a coolie would conclude he had not got the right amount, and open a discussion, which I had to cut very short; and fifty per cent. of them thought their rupees were bad, so that from all sides rose the sound of money being chinked upon the rock to test its ring. Each native, as he came up, salaamed and held out both his hands, to receive the overflowing bounty of the sahib.

"Poor people! The strongest man amongst them, who had worked in the sun and rain all the week, only took six times five annas—about equal to three shillings and fourpence; and on this, of course, many had to support a wife and children too weak or too feeble to work themselves. Then, again, the women—many of them mothers, with small, brown fragments of humanity slung upon their backs—got three annas a day, and the most they could earn was little more than two shillings a-week. Even the little children came up, ducked their small shaven heads in comical homage to the great white sahib, and held out very small brown hands for the price those hands were supposed to have earned at the rate of a penny a-day. Last of all, the maistries received pay at the rate of six or eight annas per diem; and then the horse-boys, cook, sweepers and hangers-on of all sorts. When these were satisfied, there was still a small crowd of non-contents who came up and complained that their money was bad; would I change it? which I always did when possible, as, if a poor fellow earned one rupee and chanced to get paid with a bad, unchangeable coin, there was nothing but starvation for him during the next week. Others thought there was a mistake somewhere—always to their disadvantage—and their names had to be hunted for, and the amount of money given compared with that entered in the book. It was hopeless to please them all; but on going over the accounts during the course of the next evening, I was well satisfied to find there was only an error of a few annas—happily too much given out, not too little.

" Muster and paying over, and the stores and outhouses locked up, the estate pony seen to, and his feed of grain measured out, there were still the sick and ill clustered round the bungalow verandah to be attended to before being released for the day. With these I was much helped by R——'s son, who, having spent all his life in the south of India, knows the language and habits of the natives. Between us we bandaged up half-a-dozen ulcerated legs, sewed up a chopped finger, administered castor oil and epsom salts—a horrid brew of Charlie's invention—to two babies, gave a dose of quinine to a young coolie girl who thought she had fever, and some sulphur ointment to two in-patients suffering from the itch. One old woman who had recently had smallpox came up for her daily allowance of cod liver oil. All these and many others had to be attended to before we could dine."

We have said the blood of the native is thinner

than that of the European. This shows itself in many ways. He will get an attack of fever or dysentery, it may be, and, lying down, inform his friends he is going to die; and he too often keeps this melancholy resolve, apparently lacking the resolution to hold his vital spark in. Again, he is for the most part hopelessly unambitious, except when famine spurs him, whence come much of the planter's "labour difficulties." He knows he can subsist for a week away in his own fertile plains on the amount of "raggee," "paddy," "cumboo," or other grain purchasable by four annas (equal to fivepence); and that being a day's pay on most estates, he saves a few rupees, and then returns to his hut to lie in the sun and take his daily measure of pulse amongst children and friends—an existence which fulfils all his ideas of life.

The jungle has no attraction for him unless he is kept in it by the magnetism of an Englishman's presence. It is a region of mist and terror, not only held by the fever mists, and ravaged (in his excited lowland imagination) by wild beasts, but also peopled by fearsome tribes of ghouls and goblins; no wonder he dreads the dark wooded mountains, ascends them reluctantly and quits them hurriedly (too often with his "advances" unrepaid) for hospitable and familiar plains! Times of famine tell greatly against the prosperity of an estate, for labour is then scarce, precarious, and indifferent when obtained. What "famine prices" mean to these poor people will readily be understood from the following table taken from "The Hindoo Patriot:"

Denomination of Articles.	Amount obtainable per Rupee.	
	1870.	1878.
	S. C.	S. C.
Common Rice	17 0	12 0
Best Rice	14 0	7 4
Wheat (Jowali)	15 8	12 5
Barley	26 0	16 0
Gram	12 8	16 0
Lentils—Khesari	22 0	13 0
Musoor	20 0	10 8
Kuily (Mash)	12 0	16 0
Sugar	4 14	4 8
Salt	8 12	8 0
Ghee	1 5½	1 4
Milk	9 0	8 0
Oil (Mustard)	3 4	2 10
Wages of unskilled Labourers per month	Rs. 6	Rs. 6

It will be seen that common rice, which sold in 1861 at 21 seers and in 1870 at 17 seers, sells at about 12 seers to the rupee during scarcity. This rice is of a quality chiefly consumed by the poorer classes at the rate of one seer daily on an average per head. The rice alone thus costs him every day about 1 anna and 4 pie. Add to this amount the price of firewood, vegetables, fish, oil, &c., and his two meals cost him 2 annas daily, or Rs. 3-12 a-month at the least. It will be perceived at the foot of the table that the monthly wages of "unskilled labourers" remain unchanged, that is to say, Rs. 6 per month. Such people must live on stinted rations, as many of them now-a-days unhappily do, or neglect those depending upon them.

The coolie's interest is the planter's. He should be lodged well, fed sufficiently whatever the price of grain is, and kindly treated. An estate managed on these principles will have good labour at command when other estates round about are being ruined for want of hands. Let the planter remember (whether he works in the east or west) that he and his prospects, his manners and his ways, are the subject of keen enquiry and gossip not only in the "lines" that lie below his bungalow, but all over his district, and further still perhaps; therefore let him cultivate a good repute, and when he has got his gangs together, guard them carefully.

CHAPTER IV.

PURCHASE.

HAVING attained some idea of the kind of land required to *grow* Coffee, and the usual methods by which labour for its cultivation is obtained, there come the questions as to purchase of land, taxes, surveying, accessibility (*i.e.*, roads, communications, outlets), house sites, &c., &c.

Of acquiring land there are, of course, many ways. The simplest is the permission of a native Raja, or Chief, and the subsequent selecting of such a slice of woodland as may suit means and ideas. The next simplest is when a local government gives the same permission with the proviso that the land selected shall be surveyed and the cost thereof borne by the planter; a few conditions being, perhaps, added as to roads to be opened, and rent to be paid at a future date. Either of these is, no doubt, the pleasantest way of becoming a landed proprietor known. Unfortunately, both are practically things of the past, at least as far as India is concerned. Now-a-days land must almost everywhere be rented or bought, and native sovereigns are becoming very wideawake to the value of freeholds in good districts.

Soil in private hands may be (1) bought in the rough, when particular attention should be paid to sellers' proper proofs of ownership, as many an estate is burdened during its early years with hereditary legal feuds between the ostensible owner and small proprietors—it may even be junglemen, along the borders, who persist in asserting that the Englishman's concession has overlapped their marches, and devote whole lives cheerfully to endless litigation for a worthless acre of rock or land. (2) It may be purchased ready planted, a few months established, in bearing, or practically abandoned as worn out or barren. The first two conditions will save him, of course, a lot of trouble, and he will have to pay proportionally; and as to the latter—well! a really clever planter may often pick a seemingly valueless estate out of the fire, buy it at a nominal rate, and by scientific pruning and manuring make his garden into a nice little investment. But by the time the "griffin" is able to do this safely he will be past the guidance of any books.

The following rules used to hold for the acquiring of land in various districts, and they do so still, except where they have been modified by Orders in Council, or any of those numerous local memoranda which the authorities emit from time to time, to the satisfaction of local attornies and the mystification of the public.

In Ceylon,

Those desiring Government land send their application to the Court of the Agent or chief Revenue official of the province where it lies. The specified block will then be surveyed by an official, and an advertisement inserted in the Government "Gazette," naming a day for the public sale of the tract at the Cutcherry, or Civil Court of the district, and the highest bidder above the reserve or upset price of £1 per acre becomes its freehold proprietor, without taxes or restrictions of any kind. In many cases, of course, at this nominally public "roup" there is no competition, and the applicant gets his land at a moderate price; on other occasions the rivalry is keen and speculative.

The Wynaad,

Possessing even now a bad name for fever and indifferent communication, has complicated land laws. The applicant for waste Crown land has to supply the nearest Collector with details of the hill-side he desires, its boundaries and neighbours in the way of cultivated land or pasture. Into this the Revenue Department will inquire, and if the title of the land is free and good, it is advertised and sold by auction—the upset price being the cost of survey. There is also an annual tax of two rupees an acre, compoundable by twenty-five years' tax. Land purchased here privately, from wealthy natives, or the priests of even wealthier temples, is free of this tax until it has been brought under cultivation, when the Rs. 2 per annum commences.

Through a recent copy of *The Madras Mail*, we see a new land question is engaging the attention of planters and other landowners in the much troubled Wynaad. The Government is organizing a resettlement of revenue, and at a meeting held at Vythery, Mr. Castlestuart Stuart, Special Assistant Collector, Nilgiris and Malabar, attended to explain the intentions of the authorities. He pointed out that the settlement would be for thirty years, and all lands capable of cultivation, though yielding no revenue to the occupants, will have to pay tax. The rates of assessment are not yet fixed, but probably will be settled within the next six weeks. Partial abandonment of estates after the resettlement will not be permitted; the whole of the land will be subjected to assessment, whether any portion be abandoned or not. The meeting thanked Mr. Stuart for his information, and passed resolutions thereon representing to the Government that "the existing rates of taxation are as heavy as can possibly be borne in the present state of extreme depression," and deprecating any action that would tend to increase their burdens until the views of the planters and landholders can be laid before Government.

Coorg

Once distributed its Coffee-land free, subject only to a proviso that so much should be cultivated annually—that golden period for the small capitalist is now over, and he must register his land and bid for it publicly, paying down ten per cent. of the price on the day of sale and the rest within thirty days, the reserve being two rupees per acre, including all surveying expenses.

Travancore.

Most of the land in the district has been taken up from the Travancore Government. The land is first put up to auction and sold to the highest bidder, the original applicant very often being kept out of the purchase by competition. At the last sale of lands, as much as Rs. 70 an acre was paid. This arrangement is hard on those who have at great expense and trouble selected a piece of forest, and some consideration and preference should in fairness be given to prospectors. For five years no tax is levied; after that grace, which is supposed to allow the planters to get a portion into cultivation, twelve annas an acre is charged per annum on both cultivated land and forest. A duty of a rupee a cwt. is further charged, and taking the average crops of the district at three cwt. an acre, the planter does not get off under (with interest on original purchase) four to five rupees an acre—a very high rate when what planters pay in other districts is considered. The Peermaad planters, however, have some *quid pro quo* for the highest rate they pay by having good roads all over the district, and there is scarcely an estate that could not be reached by cart. I believe the last sale of land was long ago; since then no grant has been given, and it is the present intention of the Travancore Government to dispose of no more forest land. Perhaps it is a wise decision, as in one of the most flourishing districts in the Province estates have in some cases been abandoned, and the Government is loser to the extent of the land tax, while the land probably never returns to forest again. There is an assessment also of one rupee per acre after four years, and two rupees after nine.

The estate surveyor, who has been mentioned once or twice above, is a useful personage. Often a Government official, and perhaps a half-caste, he comes up with his theodolites, note-books, and half-dozen bill-men, establishing himself in your newly-erected and very modest "prospecting" hut in the jungles. The next day he takes you half-a-mile, a mile, or even two miles it may be, up the stream, destined to work future pulping mills. That is your boundary on the west, perhaps. Thence his bill-men clear him a path and "blaze" the trees, measuring as they go to the foot of some solitary peak, henceforth the corner-post of your estate in that direction. In a few days, more or less according to the difficulties met with, he works along the ridge for a third side of your kingdom, turning homewards at the big jack tree on the spur; and then, his work done, spends a last night with you drinking prosperity to the little realm of which he has thus set the frontiers.

The price of land will vary greatly, not only according to soil, but also in regard to communications. No one likes the farthermost lots, where civilization has not penetrated and roads are unknown, whether it be in India or elsewhere, and as a consequence such blocks are usually the cheapest. If they are promising in other ways they are not to be despised, however, for Government very rarely leaves an estate upon which work is actually being done long without means of communication, and the arrival of the road largely increases the value of the pioneer estate. There is almost as much difference between the price of a garden amongst others and bounded by good roads, and a tract of as yet unopened "impenetrable" forest, as there is between a villa on the Thames and a "villa" on the west coast of Ireland! In Ceylon, the best Coffee soil has been costing £8 to £10 per acre, and £20 to £30 per acre is estimated for bringing the land into bearing, providing proper buildings, roads, drains, &c. In other countries it is far less. In Queensland, as an instance, we see by a recent Blue-book:—" Any applicant for selection of land within ten miles from the coast or a navigable river not included in the leased half of a pastoral run, who states in his application that he intends to use the soil for the cultivation of sugar or coffee, shall be allowed to select a block of agricultural land not less than 320 acres, nor more than 1,280 acres; and on proof of his having cultivated one-tenth of the land in either sugar or coffee within three years, he shall be relieved from the obligation of residence," which means the land is free to settlers. In some other places land is to be had on equally easy conditions, and in others it goes up to fancy prices.

The labour question always has a great deal to do with this. Scarcity of labourers ruined Natal Coffee; in the South American estates they are working plantations to death before "dark" labour finally sets up for itself; and in Fiji the owners are grumbling and will entirely desert those charming islands unless the ridiculous coolie laws are amended.

The intending settler would do well to look about him and gather the best information before investing his money. Better still, he should seek employment under some able manager for, say, a couple of years, when he will have learned the language, and fairly mastered the details of his business. This arrangement need not prevent his acquiring land meanwhile, or purchasing an estate if a favourable opportunity offers itself. In the latter case the work had better be entrusted to a manager, while the purchaser is gaining his experience on another estate.

"Stretch your legs according to your blanket," observes a sagacious Canarese proverb, and a little good land is a much better investment for a young man than a cheap and poor lot. There is one guide to the value of a district, an old hand hints, which may firmly be relied upon. If an estate frequently changes hands it is certainly a bad or indifferent one; if seldom, you may be pretty sure Coffee pays well, and further than that a man need give himself no concern, for hardly any landed investment pays so well in India, supposing we have little or no blight or disease, as good sound Coffee property, and people are therefore seldom inclined to part with it.

CHAPTER V.

THE NURSERY.

ACTUAL operations upon the estate begin with the formation of a "nursery," or secluded corner, where those young plants are to be reared for subsequently filling up their appointed places in the permanent fields. It is one of the prettiest and most satisfactory works the planter has to perform, as one of the earliest.

Having established himself in some sort of a hut (if he lives upon the estate—as he probably will do and certainly ought), placing the hut as much above the general level of the country as can conveniently be managed—his jungle paths roughly cut, and coolies got into some sort of working order, the next thing is to start his future plants.

The first requisite is a good piece of ground, level perhaps—or, better still, with a moderate slope in one direction, in order to facilitate natural drainage—a reasonable depth of soil, and, above all, a ready, abundant, and never-failing water supply. Let him be careful that the stream he selects is perennial, or it may fail him just when most needed. It is astonishing how completely a spell of hot weather saps the existence of a woodland torrent in the tropics. In our moisture-laden isles we know nothing like it, but under the equator, or a few degrees on either side of it, a stream that in the monsoon is strong enough to sweep away a herd of cattle, in the hot season hardly serves to find drink for a stray troop of monkeys or a thirsty sambour! Let him choose a stream, then, that holds its own against the seasons. Probably his land will be above it, on the inclining banks. In that case a convenient *ghaut* or slope and a dipping place will have to be made. But we need not say that if by the exercise of a little engineering skill—even though of amateur kind—and the erection of an embankment or two, he can get such a head of water as will suffice to bring a supply of the fluid by any rough tubing to his nursery, the labour is well spent and will repay itself many times; or he may rig up a regular water-wheel.

Mr. Robertson, of Madras, has the following observations regarding working and the construction of an admirable new " mhote," or water-lift. He says:—

" The water is raised by two leather buckets, similar to those in ordinary use in some parts of this Presidency; to each of these buckets is attached a rope which is fastened to a drum: one of these is coiled and the other uncoiled, as one bucket ascends the other descends; the drum is fixed on a rotating spindle, to which is fixed at right angles the draught bar to which the bullock is attached; the diameter and thickness of the drum varies with the depth of the well; as a general rule, for all ordinary lifts, the diameter of the drum may be equal to about one-fifth the number of feet that the water must be raised; the drum is placed about six feet above the ground, in order to allow the rope to pass over the head of the draught bullock; the spindle upon which the drum is placed is kept in its upright position by means of two beams, into which it is fixed, which cross each other at the middle, and are supported at the ends or posts placed opposite each other on the outer side of the bullock patch. The bullock walks under the draught bar attached to a curved yoke, which turns on a swivel. In raising water the bullock travels round the upright spindle, thus turning the drum and winding one rope and unwinding the other. If the diameter of the drum is as suggested, $1\frac{1}{2}$ circuits around the path will raise each bucket to the requisite height; the bullock is turned round, facing the opposite direction, while each bucket is being discharged; no longer time is required to do this than is needed for the bucket to discharge its contents." " The following may be accepted as a fair estimate of the capabilities of the machine as now ascertained :—

Cost per Day.

	Rs.	A.	P.
Hire for one bullock and driver for one day	0	8	0
Interest and wear and tear at 10 per cent. per annum on the capital invested, say Rs. 100, charged over 300 working days	0	0	6
Cost of replacing buckets and ropes three times a year, say Rs. 90, charged over 300 working days	0	4	9
Oil, &c.	0	1	0
	0	14	3

" The cost per day is therefore annas 14, pies 3. When working at the ordinary speed, 90 buckets are raised per hour; each bucket contains 30 gallons when brought to the delivery spout; the height to which the water is raised varies from 20 to 24 feet; thus, 2,700 gallons of water are brought to the surface and discharged in one hour, or 24,300 gallons during an ordinary working day of nine hours, rather more over an acre of land than a rainfall of one inch. Taking 22 feet as the average height of the lift, it would appear that the machine raises about 27,000 gallons to this height for 1 rupee."

After securing an efficient water supply, the question of soil arises. This should be of the same nature as that of the rest of the estate, and no richer in quality. It must be of the same nature in order that the young plants when moved may take kindly to it, as though the new situation were a portion of their old seed-bed, and no better, in order that they may not receive a check by going into inferior ground at an important period of their growth. A slight knowledge of geology—and every planter would benefit by such, especially in regions where there is a chance of gold appearing—will teach him how greatly soils on the outcrop of different formations can differ; so he must keep his eyes open for a good piece of land of same origin as the rest of his estate.

The nursery should be central if possible, or at all events at a point accessible to the main roads of the garden when they are made, as while it is in use much traffic will be going to and fro, and accessibility, or the otherwise, makes a great deal of difference in the account books when the cost of planting an enclosure is reckoned up.

If the planter is precise and methodical he may,

before falling to work upon the clearing of his nursery plot, calculate out to a fraction how much seed he will have to plant to cover so many acres of open land. But since there will be many failures, both in the germinating of the seed and by dying off of young plants when set out, some thousands over should be allowed for this. If of a rough-and-ready turn of mind, he may well rely upon intuitive perception in the matter.

Then commence active operations. The underwood all over the land to be cleared is carefully grubbed up and put back into the jungle, where, with a little assistance from stakes, it forms a rough fence useful for keeping wild beasts out, as they often do considerable damage, deer especially treading down the young plants. Then some of the trees must fall, if they be at all thickly set, to let in light and air to the ground beneath, and the logs cut up if possible and rolled off the ground. The fall of a tree can generally be regulated by cutting a deep notch half through it on one side, and another higher up on the opposite side. It descends on the side of the lower cut. A hundred yards by fifty yards is a good size for a first nursery. Logs, roots, big stones, and branches of all kinds moved away, and the ground cleared nicely, the beds are then marked out in preparation for digging. The only thing to be said here is that the deeper the soil is stirred the better. A broad 6-feet central path should run down the centre. On either side of this the beds strike off at right angles of any length that may be most convenient, but not more than 2 feet, or at the most 3 feet wide. "A bed 3½ feet wide by 28 in length, with plants at 4 inches apart, would contain about 1,200, or sufficient to cover an acre planted at 6 feet by 6 feet," says Hall. Their limited breadth is in order that in planting and a good deal of subsequent necessary handling the coolies may have easy and ready access to the plants without disturbing the surface.

The ground having lain fallow a day or two, the seed is put into it. For this purpose cords attached to pegs are used, the cord being stretched up and down the bed, and a furrow made with a stick by the side of it. This should be done by one of the more intelligent natives. It is astonishing what a distortion of straight lines a coolie will get into even a limited area. In this trench the Coffee bean is placed.

A regular trade is made in seed now, and there is none of the difficulty experienced in obtaining a suitable supply which was once the case. Very often a neighbouring planter is in a position to supply the necessary amount; or, if not, there will probably be natives at hand who can obtain as much as is required.

The time of planting is usually about October, and a few bushels can then always be had from the new crop just ripening. A bushel is said to contain 40,000 berries of cherry Coffee, and as most berries contain two beans, each of which germinates separately and throws up an individual plant, the number of seeds in one bushel will be not far from 80,000, from which 10 per cent. must be deducted in view of shrivelled and pea berries, leaving an effective of 70,000.* It is inevitable that some lots of seed should be less fertile than others, and it is far preferable to thin out overcrowded beds than to run short of young "stock" in a favourable planting season.

The following table may serve as a guide :—

Of Bushes permanently planted at	There will be, Plants in one Acre,	And Square Feet of Soil to each Plant,
6 feet × 6 feet	1,210	36
6 ,, × 4 ,,	1,675	26
5 ,, × 4 ,,	2,178	20
5 ,, × 3 ,,	2,904	15
4 ,, × 3 ,,	3,630	12
3½ ,, × 3½ ,,	3,555	12¼

When the planter has made up his mind as to the distances apart he intends to plant out his bushes, and knowing the number of beans in a measure of seed, he may very nicely allot his nursery space.

Though desirable, it is not often possible to make much choice of where one's berry comes from. It should, however, be from trees as healthy as

---

* Sabonadière calculates only 30,000 plants from a bushel of seed Coffee!

possible, gathered when fully ripe, pulped lightly, and then planted in its silver skin or parchment. Down the length of each bed, from end to end, furrows are made with the help of the cord and line. These furrows are, perhaps, two inches deep, and six inches of space intervene between each. In them the berries are dropped one at a time, and about three inches apart if the planter feels confident of their fertility—a little closer if he doubts it—and then the rows are carefully covered over and patted down by the women and children. Some planters recommend a layer of dried leaves to be scattered over the beds and left there until the plants are five or six inches high. There can be no doubt such a natural coverlet keeps the soil moist and cool, but the leaves harbour many harmful insects and grubs, besides a large assortment of snakes, of which the natives have an indiscriminate dread, confounding them all under one category.

If showery weather follows, the young plants will soon show above the surface—and very pretty they look as the glossy green leaves are unfolded, and thousands of slender green spikes carpet the ground under the chequered shadows of the tall trees that have been left standing for shade. When the rains that have brought them above the soil cease, it is time to commence watering. This is often overdone, we fancy, some planters flooding the beds as though they were so much rice land. A reasonable and moderate wetting is all that is required, especially if leaves are spread (as just mentioned) an inch or two thick on the soil; they will preserve it of an equal temperature and moist in a manner which any English gardener will readily understand. Much or little, the waterings must take place in the cool of the day, morning or evening; were it done under a midday sun the plants would be in danger of steaming to death, as a person would who enjoyed the luxury of the vapour-room of a Turkish bath for three or four hours! A couple of trustworthy men ought to be able to cope with this operation day by day if water is handy and the nursery not too large.

Another device for protecting young plants at this season of growth is the "pandall," or artificial cover, accepted by nearly every planter as necessary in some form or other. It is made thus:—At each corner of the beds forked sticks are put in, the forks about three feet above the ground, and from post to post are lain cross branches. Upon these in turn small boughs with the leaves still on are put, fairly thickly, and thus a shade is made for the tender plants below which can be regulated in its density at will. If branches should be scarce, then dried grass may be substituted; but it must be always remembered that "pandalls" are very liable to take fire, either accidentally or through the instrumentality of spiteful natives, and it is as well to have them as non-inflammable as possible. This artificial shading is only resorted to on the approach of the hot weather, being gradually put on as the sun dries up the moisture of the soil, keeping its place "while the sky is brass and the earth iron," and giving the tender green saplings a cool region to thrive in. When a new monsoon breaks it is gradually removed piecemeal, as now our future Coffee bushes require all the sun and sunshine that can be had through the clouds and rain to harden them off, and fit them for taking their proper place in the clearings.

In South Australia, where Coffee planting has been tried with some success, it is found that young plants thrive best under shade. "Those seeds planted in the open," says a correspondent of the *South Australian Register*, "proved utter failures, scarcely a seed being able to stand the exposure. Others planted under a very light shade coming up thinly, whilst those under very thick shade, four feet in width by two in height, succeeded admirably, as did also that sown in long sheds with vertical roofs about five feet high, open at both ends to admit a current of air. These latter sheds the manager has decided to use in future, as the grass which composes the roof is easy of removal as the plants increase in hardihood."

A danger of the monsoon that must not be overlooked is the likelihood of floods. The nursery being on a slope, it is especially liable to these catastrophes, and a strong and deep ditch should be cut sloping across the top of the cleared spaces to catch and run off any unusual downpour, while the borders of the beds should not be so deep as to keep a head of water standing about.

There is not much more to be added on this subject. The trespassing of animals must be guarded against, as well as may be, by putting strings with feathers attached from bush to bush along the outskirts, and by any other means that may suggest themselves; for it is astonishing what an amount of damage an elephant or sambour will do in a night, and most of it apparently wilful damage, if he chances to get into the nursery during his rambles. There is also a sharp look-out to be kept for rotten branches, or, worse still, whole trees coming down with a run and destroying several beds at a time. This, however, is a matter that should always be carefully borne in mind when commencing operations.

It is hardly necessary to say weeding must be always going on in the nursery if there is anything to pull up. Women and children, under a responsible maistry, do this work sufficiently well, and leave the men free for harder jobs; they are lighter and neater fingered, but want much watching and "driving." As time goes on, if the same ground is still used, as it may well be, for rearing young plants, it will require manuring with leaf mould from the adjacent jungle, and perhaps some litter from the cattle-sheds, but in any case not much of the latter.

The cost of a first nursery—clearing, bedding, draining, and planting—should not be more than Rs. 150, to which must be added the cost of seed.

CHAPTER VI.

FOREST CLEARINGS.

His nursery well under weigh, the planter—whose life is a busy one for the three first years of his estate's existence—turns his attention to the felling and clearing of forest land intended to receive Coffee plants. It will be understood that the land is everywhere uneven in Coffee districts, and overshadowed for the most part by luxuriant forests in which giant trees shoot up to the sky, and interlock their branches in impenetrable canopies, while every glade and watercourse is filled with waving reeds, wild arrowroot, or ginger; and vast tangles of creepers—many of them beautifully flowered after the rainy season—twine serpent-like over the bare rocks forming almost hopeless tangles.

The first business is to decide upon the size of the intended clearings, and the next to mark them out roughly, in order that the fellers may get to work. With regard to the best size for clearings, there are many different opinions—fifty acres is a fair plot. One set of planters hold that larger fields are much superior for many reasons. They maintain that if you have nothing less than a hundred acres in extent you enjoy freedom from the hosts of weeds which grow in the jungle, you are less troubled by harmful insects which love the shade and shelter of trees and undergrowth, and they think such clearings are more convenient and better managed. But the other side say that by making small plantations and leaving plenty of timber you gain great shelter from high winds—a thing of considerable importance to Coffee, especially in its young state—you have great stores of leaf mould within easy distance for using as manure, and they argue that, notwithstanding insects and weeds, the Coffee thrives better than in the open. Probably the best size of clearing will vary with the conditions and aspect of the estate. On windy ridges, where the young plants are liable to feel the full force of either monsoon, protection of some sort seems imperative, and none is so convenient and lasting as leaving "belts" or strips of jungle unfelled when the clearings are first made. These wind-shields should not be less than two chains through, or they will not answer their purpose; nor more, unless under exceptional circumstances, or they will take up too much valuable ground. Unless they are of fair breadth, the trees are apt to die out after a time; an eye should be kept on them, therefore, and if they show signs of getting thin, young saplings must be planted to take the place of the natural-sown trees.

Then comes the marking out. This is done with a compass and theodolite. A base line is taken wherever most convenient (along the bank of a stream, &c.), and starting from one corner of this, so many chains are measured off at right angles as may be required for the first side—due north perhaps, according to the lay of the land, and bearing in mind that it is always preferable to have the clearings full face to the wind rather than turned partially from it, so as to prevent the monsoons enfilading them. When a sufficient distance has been done for one side the line is continued at right angles so many chains for a further boundary, and then once again to the original base. For this operation, which requires only slight proficiency in the surveyor's craft, the planter needs two coolies (intelligent ones should be selected) to handle the measuring chain, another for the compass, and half-a-dozen, perhaps, of strong men with billhooks well sharpened who go on ahead and lop down the underwood, making a rough path for the Englishman, and "blazing" the trees—*i.e.*, cutting out strips of bark when he has been along with his instruments and authenticated the direction. Many a long day has the writer spent in this manner, and enjoyed the broaching of quiet valleys that no foot but the silent sambour's had ever trodden before, and the pioneering of shady hollows that had kept their repose unbroken since the beginning. Such a wealth of tree fern and pendant creeper swings overhead, and the silent birds of the forest—we have noticed most forms of animal life are silent in the deep woods—surround him on every hand; but, alas! his errand is one of destruction, he comes not to admire and withdraw, but to wage war with fire and steel.

A belt having been drawn around the doomed jungle, the trees are felled either wholly or partially. In the first case, the operation is simply one of universal destruction. It is usual to employ contract coolies for the work of demolishing. They bring up with them such cooking pots and pans and tools as they require, camping out in lean-to huts run up alongside the clearings, and remaining by their work until it is finished. Their axes are small and light by comparison to English or American weapons, but very effective in native hands. The first trees cut are along the line of the lowest ground, and then another tier above them is deeply notched, but none of these are cut through completely. Thus, perhaps, half a clearing will be treated if the day is still and windless, and then the headman goes to the highest rank of forest giants and, with a few vigorous blows, topples over a medium-sized sapling. In its fall it brings two others with it. These are matted together by rattens with more which give way, and so tier after tier rocks and swings, the strain spreading, when suddenly, with a mighty roar, the hill-side is unlaced, and a thousand years of timber go to perdition with one huge far-sounding crash. There can be no special advantage in this scene; probably it is chiefly liked as representing the highest art of woodmanship by the natives, who enjoy their work.

Necessary as this clearing is, it can be carried too far, even from the planter's point of view. Magnificent evergreen forests protecting ghat slopes have thus been ruthlessly destroyed, tremendous floods and corresponding droughts being the outcome.

The forests on the Nilgiri, Wynad, and Coorg have been rapidly disappearing during the last ten or twenty years. If this destruction is allowed to go on the Cauvery river, for instance, must in time be seriously affected. There are still vast tracts of forest, and many splendid forest-clad ravines protecting numerous streams, but what if they all go? And if there is no legislation on the subject, and no official reservation to be guarded by a responsible department, what is to prevent it? At the present rate of destruction there would be probably nothing left in another century or less.

If the felling is begun in October, then about the middle of March the forest will be ready to burn. It should not be delayed later, for about that time showers begin to fall. For months of the hottest season, the forest lies prone and withered under the fierce rays of an Indian sun. At the end of the time it is, or should be, as dry as timber can get, and not a green blade or leaf anywhere visible. The planter then selects a day with a gentle and steady breeze blowing, and going round to the windward and lowermost corner, he puts a match to a handful of dried leaves. The result is instantaneous; the fire springs up in forked tongues that enfold everything within their reach, driving back the originator of the conflagration, and then seething out into the open in a sea of crimson flame, that burns as though it would never have done for several days (if the jungle was heavy)—a column of smoke by day, and more than a pillar of fire by night; the destroying element curling up any tall, mastlike stems that may not have fallen, making them into huge torches, and finally bringing each to the ground.

If the "burn" is all that the planter could desire, it consumes everything but the very heaviest logs, and renders the clearing accessible again. He has previously taken the precaution of throwing back the light rubbish from under the "belts" of trees left as walls to the clearing, and thus prevented the fire from lapping against and destroying them. For overlooking this slight but essential safeguard we have seen many a man punished by the loss of shelter and the land spoilt for the time.

The hot white ash of the noble sal and cedar trees, worth princely sums as timber a few weeks ago, could they have been got down to the coast, now cumbers the soil, and the thick shade of the woods is turned to an open plain of desolation. If the flames have not done their work to the last twig, the clearing will need a little hand burning—*i.e.*, parties of men go and lop up with axes and billhook all the small wood that remain, destroying it piecemeal on bonfires, though this is sometimes included in the felling contract. When this has been done the land is practically ready for planting, a few heavy showers washing the ground into a more natural tint and condition.

No one can witness this reckless stripping of mountain regions without regret and some fears for the ultimate consequences. Lieut. Colonel Beddowe, in an admirable Report of the Famine Commissioners, published in their Blue-book (1884), says:—

"The denudation of forests for actual cultivation—paying assessment—has been very great during the last twenty years. In Wynad it is said to be 22,526 acres, and it has been very extensive on the Nilgiri. In the face of railways and an ever-increasing population, it must of course go on extending, and there is still ample room for much extension, though of course there must be a limit. Revenue officers will be too anxious to open out the hill tracts of their district and realize a revenue from the land, and can scarcely be trusted as to what tracts are to be reserved. These should in future be under the Forest Department, who should be responsible to Government that the water supply of the country is not affected. Coffee and Tea bushes will never protect the soil and water supply in the way that forest does; the soil being constantly broken up is washed away, and there is no accumulation of humus. Mr. Ferguson, the forest officer of Nilambur, explains the process of forest gradually turning into the poorest, most worthless scrub. He states that 4,000 to 5,000 acres are thus destroyed annually in Malabar."

Probably even the professional planter, absorbed as he is with his own immediate gains, must feel some sympathy with these sensible regrets.

The more complete the burn the easier and pleasanter is the subsequent operation of planting. A good burn is obtained by obtaining a *compact* mass of timber and branches, and firing on a suitable day before the first showers have sodden the dead leaves and damped the heavier growths. There can be no doubt it is a trying ordeal to the land at best, but in woodland districts hand clearing, as it will be readily understood, on such a scale is out of the question. By "pitting" the clearings before the burn we pocket the good soil, and save at least a large proportion of it.

Planting under shade—*i.e.*, suffering a majority of the best trees to remain standing, and not firing a clearing at all, almost always practised now in hot, dry climates, such as that of Southern India—is incomparably the most natural and rational process, though it has its drawbacks; and one of the chief is that Coffee under such circumstances does not bear so heavily as in the open. Grassland, though rarely used for our purpose, and "chena" scrub, so called in Ceylon, or land once cleared and reverting to a primitive state, of course gives less trouble in preparation.

Cingalese contractors used to undertake work at the rate of from Rs. 20 to 25 per acre, and had to be provided with tools. The rates have been reduced, and for heavy forest in the higher districts from Rs. 18 to 20 is now given, and in the low country from Rs. 12 to 15, while at the same time the men provide their own axes. Those figures will be a fair average for other Coffee countries, and include felling, lopping, burning and clearing-up, so as to leave the land ready for planting. Sometimes the planter's own men undertake the latter tasks, and then of course the estimate is reduced.

The Englishman should be careful to have a clear agreement on all contract work, *and not to over-advance the men.*

CHAPTER VII.

PITS AND PEGS.

BEFORE the actual destruction of the forest the ground has to be "pegged" and "pitted"—*i.e.*, the future position of each plant marked, and a hole dug at the spot, into which the fertile top soil is put and covered over, to save it from the scorching that follows. To delay these operations until the forest is brought down would be to render the first practically impossible, owing to the cumbered state of the ground, and the second purposeless. The first operation here is to provide an ample supply of pegs for marking the sites of the future pits. A man will find pretty constant employment cutting down young saplings of three or four years' growth. These are lopped into two-foot lengths and split lengthways into four or more pegs. A good workman is able to prepare 300 or 400 such sticks every day, piling them out of harms-way in the jungle. He will probably know the best woods to choose, but we may recommend *keena, malaboddy, doong,* or any other tree having long straight fibres.

"Pegging" is an extremely tedious operation, and one which the new hand will find very difficult in thick jungle. It consists in marking out the exact spots where every Coffee bush is to stand on a plot of woodland which has been only slightly cleared, and has been traced out by the trees, on what will eventually be the margin, having been slightly notched, or the leaves and rubbish scraped away. Supposing the space thus enclosed is fifty acres in extent and the bushes are going to stand four and a-half by five feet apart, then there will be 1,936 per acre, and some 96,800 in the clearing! The labour of marking each peg off separately can be understood.

The first thing to be done is to strike a base line right across the ground. To do this, a theodolite as previously mentioned, and two men with tall staffs painted red and white, are needed, besides trustworthy coolies, who have hold of the opposite ends of a long fifty-foot rope, divided into six-foot lengths by tags of tape or coloured rag, as well as numerous attendants with armfuls of pegs to mark the site of the holes to be dug. The Englishman then, starting from the edge of the future belt, directs the two line coolies to hold the rope taut in the direction which the instrument tells him is straight for the opposite side of the marked-out space, and as soon as this is satisfactorily accomplished the coolies stick in pegs directly under each six-foot mark. Then the line is taken forward again to the last peg, and another set measured off. This is all very well when the ground is clear and there are nothing but big trees to obstruct the view—usually a sign that the soil is good for Coffee—but occasionally there are clumps of tree fern, thickets of thorny bushes, or, worst of all, dense bamboos; and these offer immense obstacles, not so much to the base line as to those following. It may perhaps be suggested that it were useless to peg out such places as they could never be planted; but the truth is every bit of a clearing must be measured off in order that the proportion between the succeeding lines shall be ascertained.

Another sort of obstruction which makes "lining" difficult in unfelled jungle are the deep and rocky watercourses or nullahs. It does not do to stretch the measuring line straight from bank to bank, as that would distort the position of subsequent lines, but it has to accurately follow the fall of the ground, which would be an easy matter with trained English labourers, but with thick-headed natives proves a matter of great difficulty, and takes up much time. For my part, I never could see the necessity of having the lines of Coffee plants so exactly even that from any point in the clearing one can look up four neat roads, only terminated by the belts of forest; but it is the custom, and rigorously insisted upon in most estates. As this work however is difficult until it is properly understood, and a source of constant mortification to the exact when it has been mismanaged, I think I shall be justified in quoting here a very careful description of the work by *Mr. A. L. Cross*, the writer of an excellent little essay on " Ceylon Coffee."

"When a few thousand pegs have been cut in advance," he says, "the work of lining can then be commenced. The rope used in lining is generally a good stout one of three-quarters of an inch in thickness, and it should be well tarred to resist wet. Pieces of white cord, or strips of red cloth, should be inserted at the lining distance, every few feet along the rope, to mark where the peg is to be put in the ground. This is usually at intervals of five feet for the length, between each tree, and six feet for the breadth; in short, five by six, though other distances may be preferred and used with advantage. In very high and wind-blown districts five by five is a good distance. The rope having been thus prepared should be attached to a stout straight stick at each end of the line, generally a stick six feet in length, or whatever the breadth of the Coffee line is to be. A good working kangani and two men, one for each end of the rope, to hold it taut, and ten or twelve boys should then be selected, and each boy furnished with a stick corresponding to the breadth it is intended to leave between the Coffee lines. The first process is to run a base line across the clearing, generally starting from the lowest part, and as near the middle of the clearing as possible, and when that is finished and pegged out, another at right angles to it. For example, if the clearing is nearly square, thus:—

the dotted lines indicate the base lines laid down, each dot representing a peg. Of course when the lining is by unequal distances, say five by six, the pieces of cord or cloth, commonly called by the coolies the 'pû' (flower), will require to be

G

shifted to the required distance before running the second base line at right angles to the first. After the base lines have been laid down, the coolie at one of the ends of the rope should place his staff immediately alongside the first base line peg, either to right or left of the centre peg, the man at the other end of the line measuring with his staff, and the boys with theirs likewise, the same distance, to right or left of the base line as the case may be. When the measuring sticks are then in line, from top to bottom, the boys insert a peg into the ground below each 'pû' on the rope. This process is repeated till the whole of the clearing is finished. By the above method of laying down the base lines, four parties of liners can be employed at the same time, and the work done quickly. The usual mode of inserting the peg is for the boys to *drop* the peg from the 'pu,' marking the spot where the point touched the ground, and then insert it; but the best plan is to place the stick the boys use for measuring perpendicularly from the 'pu' to the ground, and insert the peg at its base. The line will be straighter. To insure this work being well done—and nothing is so pleasing to the planter's eye as to see straight lines of Coffee—it should be well looked after.

"Some planters now employ a lining instrument and staff, and these, if properly worked, ought to give very straight base lines. A row of long straight white sticks, or rather poles, placed one behind the other, and run the whole length of the clearing, will probably answer the purpose quite as well for all practical purposes. If one is acquainted with surveying, the best base lines will of course be run with the aid of the theodolite tracer. The system of using double ropes of equal length, so as to get the Coffee into squares, is quite unnecessary, and can seldom be properly carried out on very rough and broken land. The ropes used in lining should be about 160 feet in length. If the ropes are of greater length the lines are apt to get crooked. On sheltered flats lining might be done with advantage at such distances as seven by eight feet, thereby leaving plenty of room for manuring and digging round the trees, and in such situations they might be allowed to grow to the height of five feet, but so little land in the high districts is of this description that it is scarcely worth while making a difference in the lining in so small a space."

The next task calls for less personal exertion, but demands a good deal of supervision. The planter starts out each morning at daybreak, with perhaps two hundred men following in Indian file at his heels, and proceeds to the jungles already pegged and marked out. Each coolie takes with him a mammôty, an axe for cutting roots, and a long iron bar pointed at one end and flattened out into a spud at the other, chiefly used for removing heavy stones and loosening the soil. All then go to work in a long straight line if possible, but to get the hands into any sort of order in heavy jungle is much more easy to talk of than to effect, as it is not possible to see ten men at a time, and each man wants to work where the ground is softest and there are fewest roots. The daily task of each is forty or fifty pits of regulation size, and the superintendent has to see this properly done. Perhaps he places a mark where each man begins, at the last pit of yesterday's work, and then goes to the other end of the line, half-a-mile away. When he returns, he is surprised and pleased to find the first men have already finished half their tasks, but on investigating he sees the "mild Hindoos" have moved his pegs back so as to include ten or twelve of yesterday's pits, and this naturally makes him wrathful. Besides the coolies who thus scamp their allotted task, or are too sick and weak to perform it, there are many others who give a vast amount of trouble by making pits out of the straight line, or just too small to pass muster—the regulation size being two feet deep by eighteen inches square, measured across from the level of the surface of the ground. The holes should have right-angled corners, as if a tree be set in a circular hole, the roots follow the limits of the soil which has been disturbed, and become as much "pot-bound" as though they grew in stone jars; but when the pit is square the roots grow into the angles, and, finding themselves faced by walls of earth, are obliged to penetrate them and spread into the surrounding soil. By the time the pits begin to be numbered by thousands, the ground also presents a curious aspect—something as if the jungle had been overrun by monstrous land-crabs, which had dug out their underground houses in every direction; but the walking is better than usual, owing to the pits being in straight lines and the timber still standing.

After all this careful labour, the novice will look with something akin to consternation on the succeeding operation necessary in "pitting before the burn." Extravagant as it may appear, the next thing to be done, after having carefully dug these twenty-two thousand pits, is to fill them up again! The truth is, the forest under which we have so industriously scratched these holes has now to be felled and burnt, and the sufficient reason for refilling the pits is that the valuable top soil, which contains the best nourishment, might be saved from the flames, which would bake it to a brick—a result to be avoided, if possible, yet which would assuredly happen if the "pitting" were delayed until after burning. So we fill up the holes far and wide, our chief care being to see that the top soil really goes to the bottom of the pit, as the coolies are apt to scrape soil in just as it lies. After the burn, we should be able to tell the position of each pit by the earth being a little higher over it than elsewhere. The bigger the pits, as a rule, the better, since the plants have a larger amount of readily "available capital" to draw upon when first established.

Occasionally, when pressed for time, we have known the soil in the spots to be planted just levered up and loosened by crowbars, but this is a slovenly and unsuccessful arrangement. Again, another planter has been known to declare against pits of any size, maintaining that it inevitably makes the plants "pot bound," and discourages them from seeking food and moisture naturally. But ninety-nine out of a hundred planters make pits as large as their money and patience will allow.

Regarding the finances of these undertakings, pegs are cut at the rate of, say, five hundred pegs a-day by a workman whose wages are probably 5 annas. The cost per acre will depend upon the distances apart you grow your Coffee, but with the help of the table given under "Planting," you will be readily able to reckon the number of your pegs and their outlay, not forgetting to have a few hundred over for breakages, &c. Lining usually comes to a little over Rs. 2 per acre, but everything depends on the sort of jungle. In holeing, reckoning 1,500 holes to the acre, fifty holes per coolie per day, say 3,750 coolies at 6 annas, will make the expense per acre close upon Rs. 16. "Filling in"—if one man does 125 holes per day (and he cannot do more properly), then this will give an expenditure of Rs. 6 per acre.

The figures are rough, but approximate.

CHAPTER VIII.

"SHADE."

IF it is decided to grow Coffee under natural shade, such as it is accustomed to in a wild state, then the preparation of the land is a somewhat simpler work than that described in Chapter VI. There being no fire to dread, it is unnecessary to hide away a supply of fertilizing top soil. The borders of the clearing are therefore marked out as in the previous case, and a majority of trees felled, with *all* the underwood and tangle, which is grubbed up. Timber and rubbish has then to be cut into negociable sizes and moved by hand into the surrounding jungle, or rolled (a slovenly plan) into one of the watercourses which are sure to lie temptingly near.

When this has been well done, the result is a pretty bit of woodland dotted over with nice straight timber trees free from dead branches, the soil moist and cool in its natural deep chocolate hue, and the sunlight, maybe, patching it with a pavement of light and shadow as the rays come down from above—all together a prettier picture than that presented where the previously-described method is practised.

Of course, on these estates, the clearings being

never burnt, as the fire would have destroyed the shade trees, but the lighter material carried away to the borders to the last twig by hand labour, the valuable top soil of vegetable *débris* is left uninjured. That that same *débris* harbours a world of insects hurtful to the Coffee plants, which a good " burn " would kill, and also promotes the dreaded leaf disease so fatal in Ceylon, are two of the strongest arguments arrayed against the plan. Personally we have a decided leaning towards shade, "natural" or "artificial." In many countries shade is made a source of profit, and valuable fruit trees are planted between the rows of Coffee; in India neglecting to provide a shelter against the sun's rays, and some protection for the soil against the denuding effect of tropical rains, led to widespread deterioration of Coffee districts. An authority says:—

"When a planter takes up virgin forest he finds a splendid soil, covered with humus; he fells his forest and puts down his Coffee. One has only to read the numerous letters that appear in the public prints, especially those of Ceylon, which are almost entirely kept up by planter subscribers, to see how a planter's mind is exercised to keep his soil from being washed away. Look at the abandoned estates between Virajpett and Wotakuli in Coorg. Years ago the hills carried high timber forests on a rich though shallow soil on rock. But the forests attracted rain, regulated its distribution, and prevented scouring. The planter's axe levelled the trees with the ground, and now almost every planter who can get away from the place is glad to go. I do not think the rainfall is less, but the soil has gone from the hill sides. A tangled mass of weeds and jungle is springing up, and years must pass before the soil can be renewed. In Mysore I could point to an instance where the felling of 300 acres or so of a forest for Coffee resulted in the same way."

Therefore we say, shade your Coffee well—with natural shade if it is ready made to your hand, if not, grow some for yourself as quickly as possible.

Needless to say, much will depend on position, elevation, and aspect. Coffee grows well in Ceylon in the open on account of the natural humidity of the climate. In the hotter seasons of India umbrageous protection of some kind is a matter of necessity, notwithstanding the drawback of shorter crops. The amount of shade to be left where wholesale burning is not to be practised must of course be regulated according to the exposure. It need hardly be said that a great deal will be required on southern slopes, very little on northern ones, and that eastern and western slopes will require a moderate degree.

In the early years of planting in Southern India most of the managers came from an island where the climate was damp and comparatively mild, and "shade" trees consequently not essential to the culture of Coffee, as we have said. They broke up Indian forests, and, acting on their previous experience, planted their gardens all in the open, with the result that the first succession of extra dry seasons worked sad havoc amongst them. This is the explanation of those gaunt, sun-scorched gardens too common in Travancore and Mysore. Now they are wiser, and even if they do not preserve their natural protection against the sun, they make all reasonable haste to supply its place by the artificial-grown foliage of quick-growing Australian or other trees.

"I find it impossible to quit this subject of shade," remarks Elliot, in his "Experiences of a Coffee Planter in the Jungles of Mysore," "without saying a word for the numerous advantages plantations of Coffee have that can be grown under shelter of the original forest. In the first place, from the greater part of the land being only cleared at first of the underwood, and from the fact of that being burned in separate heaps, a large proportion of the soil is entirely uninjured by fire, and the valuable surface mould entirely preserved. In the next place, from the preservation of such a portion of this vegetable matter, and from the land being annually recruited by the fallen leaves, the rain water, instead of running off, washing the land, and so depriving it of a great deal of its most valuable constituents, soaks gradually into and lodges in the soil without the loss of a single drop. Thirdly, the forest trees afford shelter to innumerable birds, which are not only pleasant to see, and many of them to hear, but which are of·incalculable service as insect-eaters. Then the planter with his shade, if he does not altogether laugh at dry seasons, in a great measure neutralizes their influence by preventing the sun and wind from drying up the soil and parching the plant. And, finally, both the planter and his people can work all day and seldom feel the fierce rays of the tropical sun; and this consideration alone is of immense money value to an estate. And yet, in spite of all these considerations, we have seen shade and shelter ruthlessly cut down all over the country, and often in parts so hot and arid that it would be difficult to conceive circumstances that could be more fatal to the existence of Coffee."

In what planters term the charcoal-tree—a poor, watery, large-leafed, light-barked shrub, so called from its rising out of charcoal-littered ground—we are told we have Nature's natural shelter for more valuable timber whilst young, and all those seedlings wherewith barren spots are recovered in time. But the charcoal-tree is not quite up to the modern planter's needs. Sometimes it is suffered to grow in clumps amongst Coffee, making a better shelter perhaps than the tall grass Dutch planters leave between their rows. Usually it shares the fate of other lesser weeds in clearings, only growing on the margin of "belts" and untouched forest—a vivid green band of leaves between the soil of the plantation and the superincumbent masses of tree foliage. The older this bush gets the poorer its shade is; and though it may be of temporary service, there are other and better trees which should be growing whilst the Coffee is young. Several species answer this purpose. The most popular of them, and that with which I protected my own garden, is the Jack-tree (*Artocarpus integrifolius*), called by Tamils "Kattu Pilavoo," and in Telugu "Panasa Rurra." This tree has many good points to recommend it. First of all, Jack stands in the first class as a timber tree. The wood is a bright, clear yellow, polishing well. My first set of furniture as a "chick doree" in the jungle was after this kind, and light and handsome it looked! It stands changes of climate remarkably.

I noticed when watching native building operations that Jack-wood was used invariably for doors and their framings, and for window casings—everywhere, in fact, where it was important to have a wood which would not expand or contract with the varying seasons. Both for rough work or for fine "cabinet" uses this tree is of value, and if we *can* grow a tree of value in itself as well as *suitable to the purpose* of its planting, we may as well have it. In growth Jack equals the largest English elms, in thick jungle often running up a beautifully straight stem to the first branches. As a deep subsoil feeder, again, it acts like a powerful "pump" (if the last words of the savants are to be accepted), raising stores of moisture from deep natural reservoirs far below ground, and holding them suspended amongst its leaves for its own benefit and that of all low-growing shrubs. Demanding little or no nourishment from surface soil—a point of much importance, we need not say, as we must not import a rival in this matter to our Coffee—the numberless leaves of this tree, on the contrary, supply a perpetual top-dressing of manure; its foliage is sufficiently thick to keep out much of the sunlight, but not dense enough to prevent a pleasant circulation of air; its presence is *wholesome*; and, lastly but not leastly, the Jack fruit is a substantial pumpkin-shaped mass, weighing from twenty-five to thirty-five pounds, and full of nutritious seeds, which, roasted or boiled, are a favourite dish with the frugal natives. Thus the Jack is a good tree to grow for all these reasons. One drawback there is: it is said not to stand transplanting well. Our own method of propagation was to grow young bushes in prepared beds, remove them when twelve inches high into baskets, and plant out along sides of roads, or here and there amongst lines of Coffee in the same manner and at the same time as those plants. If the seedlings are put at distances of twenty-five or thirty feet or so, a few "failures" will not matter. Of slow growth, some planters supplement them for the first few years by castor-oil plants or bananas, both of which spring up in a few months, the former producing the first year a crop of some value, while the broad leaves of the latter are greatly valued by coolies, who prepare from them platters, dishes for rice and curry, and even drinking cups.

Dr. Shortt remarks in a lengthy report on the castor-oil tree:—

"Of several varieties the two first known as the small and large seeded are in general cultivation all over the warm countries of the world, in South of Europe and the East and

West Indies. In Southern India the castor oil is generally cultivated as an annual, with dry crops either of grain or pulse, and rarely alone, in almost every district, requiring no particular attention as a field crop. It thrives in the plains as well as on the hills to about 5,000 feet above sea level. It grows rapidly into a tall lanky plant from 8 to 15 feet in height, generally forming a large terminal spike about a foot in length, springing from the terminating branches at the summit, and sometimes two or more small side branches form, carrying smaller spikes of about 6 to 8 inches in length; each spike carries from 100 to 150 capsules which are armed with long flexible prickles and are trilocular or 3-celled, and about the size of a large marble when matured; the capsule bursts elastically expelling its seed, usually 3 in number, to a little distance from the plant.

"The small-seeded variety grows into a large umbrageous tree 33 to 40 feet in height, with a sturdy looking stout stem. Trees on my estate now measure 4 feet in girth, one foot above the soil, and 3 feet, 5 feet above the soil. It is a handsome tree, and seeds freely yielding 15 lb. of seeds per tree per annum."

The loquat tree has a fruit somewhat resembling a yellow plum. Its wood is of no value as timber, but it is a favourite as shade for Coffee in the Wynaad. I once planted a couple of hundred acres with Pepul (*Ficus religiosa*). A tree of that species was felled, and six foot length cut from the lesser branches. These, four inches in diameter, were planted firmly into the ground amongst the Coffee, and soon formed roots and burst into abundant heads of foliage. Then there is the dark green-leaved "cub-bussaree" tree, and the "goni" tree. Elliot warns us against the "taree," the "cheppul," and the "muttee." All good, suitable trees, of the many species which planters have tried, must be grown strictly in regard to the climate and needs of the soil. They may be invaluable assistants to the securing of healthy plants on the dry side of a range, and yet blight-encouraging encumbrances on the opposite or wet side, where the rain-laden clouds land and discharge their freights of moisture and mist.

CHAPTER IX.

PLANTING.

PLANTING Coffee seed directly into the clearings was at one time practised, and in such circumstances as those of small native gardens under shade, and irrigated, did well enough, but is not suited for general European usage. Then there was the importation of "stumps," and the collection of natural sown seedlings from the jungle, native gardens, or deserted plantations. All these have given way to the more regular and workmanly plan of cultivating one's own plants, as previously shown, in prepared nurseries.

When land under shade has been cleared, it is "pegged" and planted at once, damp, showery weather of course being chosen. There are several modes of performing the important operation of removing young plants from nursery to clearings. One is to scoop each seedling up with a complicated form of trowel which removes the seedling and the earth round its roots, the plants being retained in this contrivance until they are bedded out and the soil filled in round them. Another way, which seems the most certain, though also the most expensive, is to use light wicker baskets, made at

Palghat, and of the size and shape of a flower-pot. These are made of split rattan cane, and though they should be tough and elastic, it is essential they should not be so closely woven as to prevent roots of plants piercing them and penetrating the surrounding soil. It is better to have them too loosely than too well made. Into each of these a couple of handfuls of the best jungle leaf mould is placed, and then the young Coffee plants are carefully taken up with a trowel, a small piece is cut off the tap root to prevent the possibility of its being bent, and one is placed in every basket, where they may be safely left until it is convenient to plant them in the clearings. They are not moved again, but basket and all slipped into the pit, and the basket allowed to decay as it likes. This, it will be understood, is an expensive method—with this advantage, of very few subsequent "failures" occurring in the open.

If neither trowels nor baskets are used, then the plants must be taken up carefully, with as much earth on their roots as possible, transferred to their new location in shallow weeding baskets, and planted out with as little delay as is practicable. Though we have said the young plants in their bamboo transplanting baskets may be safely left about, that only applies to the wet season, when rain or overcast skies are certain; at any other time it stands to reason they would be scorched up in an hour or so if exposed to the full sunshine. Some planters adopt the plan of building rough sheds to harbour the plants when first moved into the baskets.

The number of trees that the nursery must supply depends on the distances to be between each bush. The following table will make this clear:—

DISTANCES, &c., OF PLANTS.

Feet apart.	Square Feet each.	Number per Acre.	Feet apart.	Square Feet each.	Number per Acre.
1 × 1	1	43,560	5½ × 6	33	1,320
2 × 1	2	21,780	6 × 6	36	1,210
2 × 2	4	10,890	6 × 7	42	1,037
2 × 3	6	7,260	7 × 7	49	889
3 × 3	9	4,840	7 × 8	56	778
3 × 4	12	3,630	8 × 8	64	681
4 × 4	16	2,722	9 × 9	81	538
4 × 5	20	2,178	10 × 10	100	435
4½ × 4½	20¼	2,151	12 × 12	144	302
4½ × 5	22½	1,936	15 × 15	225	193
5 × 5	25	1,742	17 × 17	289	151
5 × 5½	27½	1,584	20 × 20	400	109
5 × 6	30	1,452	25 × 25	625	69
5½ × 5½	30¼	1,440			

Thus if we plant 4½ by 4½ we shall want 2,151 seedlings per acre, and say a couple of hundred over for failures; if 5 by 5, then 1,742 will do; if 7 by 8, only 778, and so on. 5 by 5 may be taken as a good average distance, varying as suggested in a previous chapter.

"Stumps" are those plants that have thrown out their first "primary" branches. When taken out of the nursery beds their side roots are lightly trimmed and their tap roots cut off about ten inches below the green bark with a sharp knife. They grow somewhat slowly after their transplanting for twelve months, but then put on a spurt and generally outdistance seedlings that have come earlier into the clearings. Hot weather and drought affects them less than the smaller plants. Probably most managers would prefer to plant with stumps, only it will be understood they represent on high estates an extra season's growth, and it is not everyone whose nurseries are started sufficiently early to render this waiting possible.

"It should be borne in mind," Mr. A. L. Cross observes, "by planters in high districts, that nurseries sown with seed, though put in in March, would be of little use for a clearing till they were eighteen months or two years old, so that a nursery of seed put in, say, in March, 1886, would be unfit for use till August, 1887, and by that time the planting season, for plants, in districts getting the south-west monsoon would be nearly over. For the second year, if the nursery has been thinned out, the plants will be in excellent condition. I have found it best to make two nurseries the first year, one of seed, and the other of seedlings, brought from some other estate."

"Planting baskets" should be used whenever possible. Their initial expenses are often covered by the absence of "failures." The plants may be put out in the field when they have three pairs of leaves, but of course at the proper season, during the first rains of the monsoon. The advantages of the baskets are that they present little obstruction to the spread of the roots, and will be rotten thoroughly in a few months; the plants never feel that they have been removed, or have their growth stopped for a day, saving thereby a greater or less percentage of loss, according to the circumstances of the season.

Regarding the actual planting, when the plants have been gently lifted from the seed beds they are, as we have said, transported to the field in baskets, forty or fifty at a time. The work of removal and inserting in the ready holes should go on on the same day, so that the seedlings may be as short a period as possible out of the ground. Arrived at the rows, the planting coolies fill a corner of their *cumblies* with the young Coffee, which they then proceed to establish in its new home. In doing this the great things to be remembered are, that the tap root must not be bent or bruised in any way, though a few inches may be cut off if it is too long; and, secondly, side roots should be spread out as they have been growing, and not squeezed in round the stem. Sometimes this planting is done with an *alavanga*, a light crowbar, a blunt stick, the two halves of a split bamboo, the hands, or small mamotie. Probably the latter is the best and most expeditious way, but watchful supervision must be exercised in any case, for planting is one of the most important operations we have to perform.

When plants are well set in they should feel firm to a gentle upward pull, should be buried to about the same height they were in their seed beds, and should *not* be in the centre of hollow depressions likely to hold water in monsoons, and so drown the shrubs.

"Dibbling" is an indifferent method of planting wherein the soil is only loosened by the pointed end of an *alavanga* being worked round and round.

As soon after clearings are planted as possible, and particularly in the case of those deficient in shelter, it will be time to fix supports to the young transplanted Coffee trees of two years old, quickly growing into considerable bushes with thick heads of glossy dark green leaves. In spite of belts of jungle left between the clearings, the plant feels the wind more or less, and when the ground is wet it swings it round and round, so that the stem works an opening in the soil just where it comes above ground. Then, if there should be any breeze on the next hot day, when the ground is baked hard by the sun, the plant chafes against this rim, cuts through its tender young bark, and very speedily dies. So we have to provide a support by driving in a three-foot stick, sloping towards the plant from the direction of the south-west monsoon, and firmly but gently tying them together with a thin rattan fibre or any stringey bark which grows wild in the jungles, the fibre being crossed between stake and plant to make a manner of cushion. "Supplying" or filling up of failures should be more carefully attended to, from time to time, than it is on many estates. Opening new land while the ground already brought "under cultivation" does not carry anything like the number of plants it might and was intended to is, we need not say, foolish in the extreme. Managers occasionally push forward and take up fresh forest when as much as twenty per cent. of the Coffee behind them is dead or useless. This is profitable to no one, and least of all to those over-eager shareholders at home who are usually at the bottom of the unwarranted "extension." Failures may be divided into two classes—the inevitable and the accidental. The first occur because the young seedling has been put out over slab rock through which its roots cannot penetrate. There is nothing to do but submit in such cases. The next class is open to remedy, the young plants having died because their tap roots have been doubled up, because rats, or grub, or grasshoppers have been at their tender shoots, or from rough handling by the transplanting coolies. Perhaps there is a boulder as big as a plate at the bottom of their "pit." A little enquiry is nearly sure to explain the reason of gaps in rows of Coffee; and unless it is rock underneath, or something of the kind, a new plant nicely installed will well repay the trouble of investigation and repair. Nothing has been said about roads, as they will be noticed presently; but a good path properly kept along the edge of jungle is an invaluable barrier against weeds, an important aid to locomotion, and hence tends to keep down expenses.

These expenses may be indicated thus: If on a hundred acres we have 187,500 plants, and these are planted at the rate of 250 per coolie per diem, then 750 coolies at 5 annas will be Rs. 234, 6 annas. Then, carriage from the nursery and on the field, pruning roots, &c., at the rate of one coolie to every 10 planting, say 70 coolies at 5 annas=Rs. 21, 14 a.

Suppose out of the above number we have to "supply" 20,000 plants, 80 coolies per acre at 5 annas per day=Rs. 25, will get in the new stock. If plants or "stumps" are bought from neighbouring estates, they may generally be obtained at about Rs. 4 to 5 per 1,000 fit for putting out.

Bamboo baskets, 9 inches deep and 6 inches wide at the top, can generally be made for Rs. 10 per 1,000 in lowlands, but up-country planters have to pay as much as Rs. 15 per 1,000 for these planting baskets.

The distance from nursery to clearing, the nature of soil, whether men or women are employed as carriers, the method of planting, the size of the bushes, and condition of the ground in regard to roads, will all affect such estimates.

CHAPTER X.

WEEDS.

WEEDS are almost universally recognised as amongst the worst of planters' foes. We have no ambition to join the standard of revolt against this orthodox opinion which one gentleman at least of Ceylon experience has raised, yet we have never felt quite satisfied with the bare sun-scorched surface of earth the energetic weeder leaves behind him. We have often been tempted to ask, is there any single instance in Nature (and we have a great respect for Nature!) where bush or tree in a tropical climate springs from a bare and naked soil? Even if a few such instances could be pointed out, it cannot be denied that a natural manner of growth is first a carpet of low grass or herbage, through which these better and bigger bushes and trees force a way. Even in dense, dark woods and jungles, where there are practically no weeds, a thick blanket of twig and fallen leaf supplies the place and answers the same purpose. Scrape a little of this aside and we shall notice fine fibrous roots of big plants, close under the skin of matter, lying in every direction; place the hand upon this newly exposed surface and it will strike cool, and more or less damp, in the hottest weather. If we turn up a mat of weeds, even though their surface is fully exposed to the sun, yet the soil beneath them will be wonderfully fresh and pleasant.

Coffee has proved itself to be an exhausting growth; all trees or plants which are kept without undergrowth and weeds must be so, as whatever they yield in fruit or leaves is removed. Jungle fertilizes itself by the leaves and rotten *débris* of ages. "Keep the jungle quite clean below, and you would soon see how even scrub would, in ten or twenty years, grow feebly where Nature sows her seeds and reaps her fruits for consumption on the premises—nothing is lost. No doubt heavy manuring will give you crops of anything for a time, perhaps occasionally for ever, but *people will not make fortunes out of land that requires it.*" Still! we weeded our own estates according to the prevalent fashion, and can only advise that if we must destroy the natural protection of the soil we should encourage good and substantial shade for it, with careful draining across the slopes. When land has been burnt, for the first two or three months there are practically no weeds to contend with; but after the first rains they appear, straggling out from the surrounding jungles, creeping up from watercourses, and stealing along under shelter of the great fallen logs. Then is the time to keep the upper hand of them. Once let skirmishers of the advancing army enter into undisputed possession of the ground and practically they will make it all their own.

At such times hand-weeding is generally sufficient; and if the head man or maistry can be relied upon, women and boys will do the work very well, while more cheaply than men, whom they excel also in the necessary art of pulling up the weeds root and branch, so that there shall be nothing left to germinate. If, however, labour has been scarce, as it will be at times, and the surface of the estate begins to show visibly green with uninvited vegetation, then resource must be had to "mamoties," implements something between a Dutch hoe and a light spade, with the blade set at right angles to the short and straight handle. Men are required to wield these, of course, and the day chosen should be one of sunshine, so all weeds may wither directly they are hoed up. Not more soil than necessary should be drawn away from the stems of the bushes, nor indeed should the land be deeply disturbed at any time under this system of "no weeds," for rains then carry away the fine fertile tilth much more readily. Fear of loosening and so losing the mould should always make us weed by hand when it can possibly be managed.

Whatever our mode of weeding is, the workers keep between their own rows of Coffee, and thus maistries, who walk to and fro upon the land passed over, can see how work has been done, and promptly discover and send back any delinquent found guilty of leaving growing anything but Coffee behind him.

The plants that steal out from the jungle and spring into life amongst the trim rows of Coffee, with the wonderful spontaneousness of tropical vegetation, are many and various. "White weed," "Spanish needle," and common bracken fern are amongst those most troublesome and widespread, though every district usually has its own special kinds. Should any of these be rampant (and I have seen them matted into an almost impenetrable breast-high cover!) then it will be difficult to remove them off the ground. They must be buried in long trenches between the rows of plants—a long, troublesome, and costly work—or burnt in heaps on the roadways. The bracken is one of the worst of weeds, and is identical with the English form. The new hand is surprised to find himself, though under the tropics, knee-deep in fern, and surrounded by mountains and torrents, all exact counterparts of far-away Scottish or Welsh scenery.

For disposing of small weeds, it is a good plan to have square holes of say 5 ft. by 5 ft. at distances of 250 yards along the lower sides of the roads. Into these all weeds are tumbled from the gathering sacks and trodden down. Finally, the whole art of weeding may be said to lie in the simple formula—*to begin early and keep on at it.*

In general this operation has to be done twice

a-month—less often in the hot weather and more frequently in the monsoon. The cost will vary exactly in regard to the amount of work, but if an estate is in good order in this respect, two monthly weedings, costing from fourteen annas to one rupee per acre, should keep it free and nicely clean.

CHAPTER XI.

PRUNING.

THIS operation, entirely an artificial one, has for its purpose, firstly, the keeping of Coffee trees at such a height that the crop may be readily gathered; secondly, cutting them down for protection against wind on exposed slopes; thirdly, to let light and air into the bushes; and, fourthly, to select such wood as is best fitted to produce crop, and for the discarding of most of that which would run to leaf only, or is past bearing.

"Handling" is an intermediary form of pruning—pruning, in fact (for the most part), without a knife—when fingers and nails are used for the selection of young buds likely to make well-placed and fruitful stems and the removal of surplus shoots.

There are none of those essential works that have not given rise to contentions amongst planters, with whom all sorts of theories are rife upon the subject. Under the first section comes the question of what height we are to allow bushes to grow, in order that they may cover our ground nicely with spreading branches, and we yet be able to gather their ripe crop cheaply and expeditiously. The largest-bearing extent of plant is also required which can be safely carried in view of the prevailing winds.

In American States, as a rule, Coffee bushes are allowed to grow far taller than in India or Ceylon. They overtop the stature of a man at maturity, and thus their crop has to be gathered from stageings, a plan that does not recommend itself to English planters. Grown, as they generally are, in sheltered hollows, they may be allowed to reach any height with safety as far as wind is concerned, but in our own possessions plantations usually occupy slopes of wind-swept hills; hence "toping" at a moderate distance from the ground is essential. Perhaps, where wind is likely to be strong and soil is not very rich, 2 ft. to 3 ft. may be regarded as a judicious height to arrest further upward growth by removal of the topmost bud of the main shoot. "In a sheltered situation, where the soil is good and the climate moderately warm and humid," says Hall; "in other words, under conditions the most favourable to the growth of the Coffee tree, a maximum height of 5 ft. may be adopted. It must be remembered, however, that very rarely is such a combination of favourable circumstances to be met with, and that, consequently, this will not be found a suitable height." The opposite extreme is when planters cut their bushes on monsoon-swept ridges down to 18 inches, with very satisfactory results, it is said; though for our own part we should hardly care to plant such land, or, if it were planted, should try at once to cultivate some sort of shelter-belts around the unfortunate garden.

From 2 ft. to 5 ft., then, is the range of Arabian Coffee on the hills of Ceylon and Southern India; it being borne in mind that by topping we induce a tree to throw out lateral branches for crop bearing, and keep it within a reasonable "get-at-able" size. Regarding Liberian Coffee, one manager in the low country of Ceylon says he holds topping these trees at all to be a very objectionable operation. The common Coffee plant can be forced into an artificial form without sacrifice of any crop, because there is a period, longer or shorter, between crop and blossom, in which old wood can be eliminated; but he does not very clearly see how artificial form is to be advantageously imposed upon a tree that carries its full crop all the year round, and on which pruning can only be carried out at a sacrifice of crop. One object of forcing Arabian Coffee into artificial shape is to get the whole growth under hand, whereby facilitating and cheapening the gathering of crop; but the average Liberian tree puts out its first branches at a height of stem little short of that at which the Arabian plant is usually topped, so that this end cannot be answered by topping at 6 or 7 ft. High trees planted close together are apt to be thin and unproductive about their lower branches. These often are little more than long twigs, tagged with a leaf or two, thus making the "umbrella trees" of deserted nurseries and abandoned plantations. They have to be reduced within reasonable stature, and very carefully *handled* subsequently. Bushes, on the other hand, unduly dwarfed, may, if necessary, be allowed to fulfil their natural propensity to rise, one, the strongest of the many green, rapid-growing suckers always thrown out, being selected as a new ascending axis and the others rigorously suppressed.

"Plants should be topped as soon as they have reached the desired height. At this stage of their growth this can easily be done by a pinch between the finger and thumb nails. As, however, some plants will be found more forward than others, a knife will be required for use in cases where the wood is more matured. Each coolie should be provided with a measuring stick cut to the proper length, and holding this against the stem of the plant, be instructed to snip off the pair of young primary branches next above the stick at about an inch from the stem, the latter being then also cut off above them. By this means the joint or point of union of the amputated branches will form a sort of band, and prevent the stem from being subsequently split by weight of the next branches pendant on either side when laden with crop." Checking the upward growth is only a first business; the next is that of "handling," or, in other words, removing while still young and tender all those shoots growing crossways in the tree or growing too near the main stem. The Coffee bush, as nature meant it to be, is a beautiful sample of order and regularity. From the straight central trunk shoot out at regular distances pairs of branches which grow from opposite faces of the stem, each pair making a cross with the one above it; thus, if the first two point respectively east and west, then those above them will be north and south, the next east and west again. These are the *primaries*, and botanically their arrangement is described as alternate and opposite—a method of growth ensuring each leaf as much light, air, and room as possible.

Three or four inches from their juncture with the trunk they in turn give rise to opposite pairs of *secondaries;* but these lie all in the same plane with the surface of their leaves to the sky, and their under part to the ground. This may tend to make some of our sentences better understood.

In handling—an operation which should be done at regular intervals, and may well precede monthly weedings in the clearing—we remove first of all all *suckers* arising from the ground or stem, all branches tending to grow out of their true direction, and lastly, all those buds on the primaries within six inches of the main stem about to produce secondaries if left alone. By this means is secured a clear space of a foot in diameter down the middle of the tree, light and air let into it, and our prospects of a good, abundant, and healthy series of crops greatly increased.

So far the work of the pruner is simple enough: it is on the question of general pruning, before or after crop, and the lightness or heaviness of the operation, that opinions vary.

Mr. W. D. Bosanquet, a well-known Ceylon planter, has recently made some sensible remarks on the subject, which we think deserve quotation:—

"In high districts Coffee *wood* takes from nine months to a year, sometimes even more, to arrive at maturity. In the days before leaf disease, the difference of opinion was one between pruning before or after the blossoming season, with the object of assisting the wood either to increase its blossom, or else to bring its crop on after the blossom had set. Now our main endeavour is to help the trees to set their blossom, and if this is attained we can help the trees by the aid of manure. The effect of pruning is to cause the tree to throw out a fresh flush of wood, and from this wood is selected in the ordinary course that which is to bear the following crop.

"Now if your pruning is done early—*i.e.*, before the 15th say of April—and your wood is accustomed to mature in nine months, you are really just at the right time, whereas by pruning after the blossoms are over the wood subsequently formed would still be green in the beginning of the following year. If a late pruning is adopted systematically then it must be necessary at the time of pruning to leave on the trees such wood as has formed before the blossoming season commenced, as in an ordinary blossoming season the formation of new wood should be checked, and the old wood be hardening: your late pruning is therefore adopted with the view of giving your wood at least twelve months in which to mature. In the majority of cases I should give my verdict for early pruning, and for this reason, that where Coffee is intended by nature to grow there it will in ordinary seasons mature its wood in nine months at the most; still if I had to deal with an estate where the longer period was required I should then prune late, but, guided by the balance of probability, I should at the same time hasten to substitute for the Coffee some cultivation better suited to the climate.

"Whether the pruning should be heavy or light is a very important question, and I feel here that I am treading on delicate ground. It is certainly necessary that the pruning should be adjusted according to the power of the tree to make root, for it is to this power of the tree to make root below ground that it will owe its ability to form wood above, and in these days of leaf disease and wet seasons the root development is only too much checked already. The amount of leaf on the tree mainly determines the development of root, for the evaporation or transpiration from the leaves is the cause of the suction exercised by the roots on the soil. If therefore you unduly reduce your foliage you reduce the power of the tree to nourish itself from the fertilizing matters of the soil. In a strong soil this is not so much the case and may be an advantage, as the upward flow is not immediately checked by the reduction of the foliage, and consequently there may be a concentration of food material in the roots which, when fresh foliage has formed itself, will afford extra nourishment to the tree if carefully regulated by the subsequent handling. Prune therefore according to the strength of your soil as evidenced by the vigour of the tree, and pay the utmost attention to the after handling.

"Handling I look upon as the most important work upon the estate as being the real regulator of the crop. Too often I notice the inferior labour of the estate turned on to do this work. By the handling you direct the strength of the tree into right wood. The handling after the pruning is the time when you select the wood which is to bear the following crop, and no more wood should be left on the tree than it has the power to bring the crop of to maturity. At this time, therefore, you cannot give too much attention to the work, and all your subsequent handlings should be directed towards the same object—viz., turning the strength of the tree into the wood you have reserved for crop. In conclusion, what we require is the training of our faculties of observation: a few simple observations such as marking the branches at the time of blossoming, or the watching of the wood from the time of its formation to the time when it has borne its crop, and the noting down the result will lead on to making further observations, and the comparison of notes among ourselves will add to the mass of general information. But above all things have in you a reason for what you do founded upon accurate experiment."

This work, in fact, requires care and a knowledge of the estate, and what may be looked for from it in the way of nourishment for the trees. Pruning in gardens where the handling has been constant and careful will be a much lighter and pleasanter work than where it has been neglected.

Should the planter come into charge of bushes never under the knife, and are almost hopeless tangles of twig and branch, he should then proceed cautiously, clearing out the centre of the tree one year, and removing all suckers from above or below, while the next year he may select his crop-bearing wood and take out all cross-growing and superfluous material.

In all pruning operations it should be remembered that roots and leaves are intimately related, and anything the one experiences will be inevitably felt by the other.

"Toping" can be done for Rs. 2 per acre, and the work should be carried out just as the green bark is turning brown. Pruning and handling will probably come to between Rs. 10 and Rs. 14 per acre.

CHAPTER XII.

ENEMIES.

THE profits derived from healthy Coffee are so large, that were it not for many enemies which hamper the planter's struggles and stultify his best efforts, his occupaion would be one of the most profitable in the world. As it is he has to contend with numerous foes, and the more lowly and minute forms have proved themselves the most difficult to combat in those long struggles which have been waged since Coffee cultivation rose to its present importance in the various territories of the Crown.

From the mammalian kingdom he has not much to fear, or is generally able to devise efficient remedies against their ravages. Amongst

ANIMALS,

Elephants and hill *buffaloes*, as well as domestic *cattle* of natives, sometimes do considerable damage. *Deer* of all kinds, and particularly sambour, common to every part of India and Ceylon, roam in wooded districts, often coming out of an evening into the planter's coffee or guinea grass clearings to browze upon what they can find. This is chiefly in remote and newly opened forests, where their visits afford the Englishman a chance of a little sport at his doors after the day's work is done—a successful shot stocking his larder with very good venison, and its echoes effectually scaring off, for a long time, the remainder of the herd. *Jackals* and *monkeys* take a few of the sweet, ripe Coffee fruit, but so small a quantity as to be insignificant. Not so the *coffee rat* (*Golunda Ellioti*). This quaint little animal is sometimes an enemy of importance. Its usual habitat is in the jungle, but when pressed by hunger it comes forth and fares, no doubt luxuriously, on the buds, blossoms, and bark of the planter's bushes. If twigs are too slender to bear its weight, it nibbles them through and enjoys the feast upon the ground. The young green bark is eaten, the leaves dragged into the underwood and used for nests. These nests, placed in a thick bush, are about 6 or 9 inches in diameter. " Round and round the bush," Sir Walter Elliot says, " are sometimes observed small beaten pathways, along which the little animal seems habitually to pass. Its motion is slow, and it does not seem to have the power of leaping and springing by which the rats in general avoid danger. Its habits are solitary and diurnal, feeding in the mornings and evenings."

Dr. Jerdon, of Nellore, remarks:—"Yanadees of Nellore catch this rat, surrounding the nest bush and seizing it as it issues forth, which its comparatively slow action enables them to do easily." According to Sir Emerson Tennent, " The Malabar coolies are so fond of their flesh that they evince a preference for those districts in which the Coffee plantations are most subject to their incursions. They fry the rats in cocoanut-oil, and convert them into curry." Kellaart says that on one estate alone, and on one day, a thousand have been killed. Their migrations in search of food are like those of the Scandinavian lemming. Poison and traps thin their numbers, and trench-pitfalls, broader at the bottom than at the top, eighteen inches deep, destroy many at times. They seldom eat the ripe Coffee berries. Probably there is no way of clearing an infested plantation so good as once a-month forming a long line of coolies, each coolie armed with a stout two-foot stick, and regularly beating through Coffee and belts. The natives will thoroughly enjoy this, and it is not expensive.

Flying foxes are sometimes troublesome. To guard against their depredations one planter suggests taking a light wattle stick or bamboo—" Fix a little paint-brush to the end in a transverse direction; then have a pot of coal-tar prepared. Dip a little of it, and touch the leaves here and there about the trees where the animals are likely to settle. The tar will not hurt the trees. If some pyroligneous acid be added to the tar it will be all the more effective, on account of the stronger smell. The tar and acid must be heated considerably in order to make them combine." The same may be said of a species of the delightful little palm squirrel (*Gilehri*, in Hindi; *Beral, Lakki*, in Bengali; *Alalu*, in Canarese; *Vodata*, in Telegu), which comes up after the monsoon and takes a small per-centage of Coffee cherries, leaving the undigestable seeds in its track along logs and branches. Few birds are accused of doing damage to Coffee. On the contrary, most species should be encouraged by every possible means (a view, we are glad to see, that has just been accepted by the Ceylon Planters' Association), for they are undoubted destroyers of much undesirable insect life. Amongst the

INSECTS

Are some of the worst foes the planter has to reckon with. One of these, "the grub," is the fat yellow larva of a species of cockchafer, a creature doing much harm even in England. One Superintendent writes as follows:—

"The instinct and voracity of these creatures are marvellous, for they will destroy and greedily devour almost any vegetable or animal substance they fall in with, and they have a wonderful faculty for selecting first, as food, that which is most palatable to them. Coffee rootlets seem to be their special weakness; but even the bitter rootlet of cinchona, in the absence of the former, is not despised by them, nor is that of grass and almost every description of weed. I am told that they will not attack the roots of tea bushes, but of this I am very sceptical, and, were I planting it where I knew they existed, I should adopt every possible means of reducing their numbers. In dealing with this pest, we should be content with a patient and persistent course of ameliorating measures. The well-known applications of lime and salt as insect destroyers might be tried with hope of success."

To destroy them utterly he says:—

"This can be accomplished by applications of fertilizers obnoxious to the insect, dug broadcast into the soil. In spreading the manure over a larger area we not only induce a larger root surface, but we reduce the chances of every rootlet being reached, and make grub life harder.

"From constant communication with the Entomologist for the Royal Agricultural Society of England, and through experiments carefully conducted here, I have come to the conclusion that rape cake, in which mustard seed forms a considerable proportion, is a remedy as well as a valuable manure, for I have found it is the only substance of the kind that they cannot exist on. Castor and cocoanut cake they seem thoroughly to enjoy."

Recent issues of the *Ceylon Government Gazette* contain a correspondence on this " grub " which ravages the Coffee plantations of the island. The principal, and in fact only important, document is a lengthy report by Mr. R. McLachlan on the subject. Some forty species of beetles were submitted to him, but special interest centred in twenty of these, all or nearly all of which were allied to the *Melolontha vulgaris*, or common European cockchafer. Mr. McLachlan assumes that no undergrowth of grass or other herbaceous plants is allowed in the plantations, for the grubs of the European cockchafer and its allies feed on the roots of such plants, and not as a rule on those of trees and shrubs. But the larvæ would make their way from the roots of the weeds to those of the Coffee plant. Whether hardening the surface of the ground around the plant, so as to render it difficult for the female to deposit her eggs, would be of any efficacy is a point for the planters to decide for themselves in view of the welfare of the plant at the time. Mr. McLachlan professes himself unable to suggest any chemical poison for the grub, although he thinks that dilute kerosene oil might be tried. He advises, "above all things," to encourage insectivorous birds to the fullest possible extent, and adds that a flock of crows probably destroy more grubs in an hour than would be possible by any artificial means in a week; the systematic catching of the perfect insect or larva is also suggested as beneficial, and hand-picking should be resorted to where labour is cheap.

G. F. Halliley, the "Champion of Weeds," says:—

"Weeds are a perfect cure for grub. A few years ago, the upper part of Maria Estate (Lindula) was very bad with grub; the proprietor allowed it to get rank, so that the grub should have something to feed on, and not eat the roots of the Coffee, and the cure was perfect. If we are not allowed to *cultivate* the green crop for Coffee that Nature provides, then Indian corn is the next best we can grow, provided the stalks are buried before the pods form, but 'white weed' kept in bounds is undoubtedly the best. In former years, if one looked at the back of a healthy Coffee leaf, he could see with the naked eye the tiny mouths along the midrib, wide open, sucking in the humus arising from the weeds. Look at a leaf now, and all that can be seen are a few knots. The humus was kept up in dry weather by the fall of dew at night."

Then there is the *white or mealy bug*, and the *brown or scaley bug*. The first *(Pseudococcus Adonidum)* is of a light, dirty brownish colour and slightly downy. Both larva and pupa are active, *i.e.*, move about. Propagation goes on amongst them all the year round. They affect hot dry localities, and are found not only on the branches of the trees, but also on the roots to a depth of one foot. The white bug of the Ceylon Coffee trees seems to be identical with the species which is neutralized in the conservatories of Europe.

The *brown, black or scaley bug (Lecanium Coffeæ)*, is a minute, dark-coloured insect, attaching itself to the tenderest shoots of plants; "the females have the appearance of small scallop shells adhering to a leaf or twig in the same manner as a scallop to a rock. In a short time the whole of the green wood of the tree will become covered with these, and coated over with a black, soot-like powder, which is an excretion of the insect." These bugs are usually most troublesome at elevations of 3,000 feet in cold, damp localities. They have a host of enemies and parasites of their own amongst the *Hymenoptera*, yet contrive to thrive amazingly when once they get a footing in a plantation. 1843 is said to have been the date of their first appearance in Ceylon. All that the planter can do to check their ravages is to dust each tree, on the first appearance of the blight, with a mixture of pounded saltpetre and quicklime in equal parts; or he may set intelligent coolies to brush over them with a mixture of equal parts soft-soap, tar, tobacco, and spirits of turpentine. This may do some good.

Then we have the *borer* (*Xylotrechus quadrupes*), a pretty and interesting beetle to the entomologist, but a thing of dread to Coffee owners. It is a longicorn beetle of the family of *Clytidæ* represented in England by the active wasp-beetles often seen on sandy banks and warm palings. In colour the Indian specimens are black or very dark brown, with light yellow or white bands running transversely across their elytra, making when the wings are closed V-shaped marks. The four posterior femora are of a pink colour. This beetle, which destroyed hundreds of acres of Coffee in Coorg during 1865 and 1866, and has been ever since more or less destructive, lays its eggs on the stem of Coffee shrubs usually in weedy and neglected plantations a few inches above the ground. When these have been hatched the young "caterpillar" works its way into the stem of the plant and drives a burrow up through the pith, thereby effectually killing the plant. C. P. Hull's statement that the beetle eats a way into the plant *and deposits its larva there* is entomologically inaccurate. If the trees attacked are pulled down sideways they snap off at the point where the grub inside commenced its upward progress, and the only thing to do is to burn them and their intruder, replanting the vacancy or suffering the stump to throw up a sucker, which it will often do. Dr. Bidie thinks "shade" is amongst the best remedies we have for this pest, not so troublesome now, however, as it was some time ago.

Certain *weevils*—members of a very world-wide and everywhere destructive order—occasionally do damage on the estates, especially one small brilliant green species which covers acres of plants and eats up every leaf. P. L. Simmonds' statement, again, that it is "two and a-half inches long by one broad," we take it, is a slip of a generally cautious pen.

Besides these beetles there is the *white ant*, which plasters our bushes up to their crowns with hard mortar, effectually smothering them. In some districts it is unknown, in others it is a dreaded foe. Although white ants, says the *Friend of India*, are a pest as much to certain crops as to anything else, they are said to perform a service to agriculture on unoccupied ground similar to that performed by the earthworm in England. They are specially destructive to sugar-cane, and have actually been the cause of stopping the cultivation of the cane in several *pergunnahs* of the Cawnpore and other districts. Mr. Ridley, of the Lucknow Horticultural Gardens, however, has found a remedy for the depredations of the white ant in the field which he has proved invaluable. Kerosine oil will not of itself mix with water, but if first shaken up with milk it will amalgamate with that, and can be then diluted with water to any desired extent. A little of this mixture, we are told, goes a long way, and proves a very effective insecticide. A mixture of two parts of oil to one of sour milk, "churned" together, mixed completely, and this mixture diluted to the extent of one wineglassful to four gallons of water, will not injuriously affect either plants or grass, but will effectually keep off white ants. Carbolic acid and also coal tar have been tried at different times with very partial results. Coal tar poured hot into their holes, and mixed with the material of the ant hill, is more effectual and lasting than carbolic acid, and is less costly. But to destroy them some method of poisoning must be resorted to. M. C. Road, of Hudson, Ohio, says ants may be destroyed by the following application:—Mix thoroughly one part of Paris green in four parts of flour, and stir the whole into such a quantity of molasses as will run into the small holes in the ground in the ant hills. Most of them will be poisoned by the first application, and one or two more in a few days will finish the work.

It may serve the experimenting planter to know in this connection that the three most important and valuable materials now in common use as insecticides in the United States are—

(1) Arsenical Compounds;
(2) Emulsions of Petroleum;
(3) Pyrethrum.

1. *Arsenical Compounds.*—Paris green and London purple may be used in suspension in water in the proportion of from half-a-pound to one pound of the powder to forty gallons of water. When mixed with flour or other diluent the proportion should be one part of the poison to twenty-five or more of the diluent.

2. *Petroleum Emulsions.*—A satisfactory emulsion may be made in the following proportions: Kerosine, 1 quart; condensed milk, 12 fluid oz.; diluted with water, 36 oz. This is emulsified by violent churning, and before use it may be diluted with water from twelve to twenty times. Equal parts of kerosine and condensed milk may also be thoroughly mixed or churned together, and then diluted *ad libitum* with water.

3. *Pyrethrum.*—Pyrethrum can be applied (1) as dry powder; (2) as a fume; (3) as an alcoholic extract, diluted; (4) by simply stirring the powder in water; (5) as a tea or decoction. As a powder it may be mixed with from ten to twenty times its bulk of wood-ashes or flour, but before use should

remain for twenty-four hours with the diluent in an air-tight vessel.

Again, the ant-tormented Englishman who can procure "Little's Chemical Fluid" might be told that when a portion of one of the yards at the sheep quarantine, Indooroopilly, was attacked and partially eaten away by the white ant, the quarantine keeper poured a bucketful of liquid from the sheep dip on one of the posts, and, noticing that the ants drop dead immediately on coming in contact with the liquid, he applied it to all the posts and rails that had been attacked. After a considerable number of weeks had elapsed, the fencing was thoroughly examined and found perfectly free from the ants. The liquid used in the dip was Little's Chemical Fluid, mixed in water in the proportion of one of the fluid to 100 parts of water. The price of the fluid, wholesale, is only 8s. 6d. per gallon, so that if it is found to be effective, there can scarcely be found a cheaper remedy.

Grasshoppers amuse themselves by shearing off the young shoots and buds; while the *coffee mite (Acarus Coffeæ)*, closely allied to the "red spider" of Europe, though hardly perceptible to the naked eye, yet withers the foliage of whole hill sides at a time. "It feeds on the upper side of the leaves, where, amogst the live insects, empty skins and minute red globules are found in plenty. These globules are fixed by a style to the leaf, and are the young in the first stage of existence; the style is the mouth, but the rest of the body is a perfect globule without any appendages whatever. These latter, however, gradually break forth, and when the animalcule is furnished with all it requires, it lets go its hold."

Larva of many lepidopterous insects also do much harm, especially in some South American and West Indian districts.

Fungi.

All these drags on the planter's prosperity, however, sink into insignificance by the side of a minute and consequently intangible fungus. The leaf disease (the *Hemileia vastatrix*) made its appearance in Ceylon in 1870. The effect was felt when the very next crop came to be gathered. But for some time to come the disease only appeared every other year, and there were alternate seasons of good years and bad. At first every effort was made to fight it. Quacks and professors were alike consulted; but the experts from Kew Gardens were able to do as little as Mr. Eugene Schrottky from Bombay. In 1856, when the Coffee plants in Ceylon may be said to have been in their pristine vigour, the average crop of berries per acre was 5 cwts.; latterly, owing to the ravages of the disease, it is only $2\frac{3}{4}$ cwts.; that is, the profitable margin of the crop has disappeared. There is now, of course, much more land under Coffee than there was in 1856. If the same rate of productiveness had been continued, Ceylon should now have yielded something over a million cwts. of plantation Coffee. The present yield is not half that amount. A recent island crop of Coffee was only 436,991 cwts., being less than that of any previous year since the disastrous year 1854, which is talked of in Ceylon very much as the year after the Bombay Share mania is talked of here. The export of beans in 1881 was 219,674 cwts. less than 1880, and 361,344 cwts. less than the average export of the previous ten years. At the customs' rate of Rs. 50 per cwt. this would be an annual falling-off of Rs. 1,80,67,200.

There are other reasons, unfortunately, in addition to the leaf disease to prevent the Ceylon planters taking a cheerful view of their position. The estates best suited to Coffee have been worked out. There is now no such soil left as when the districts of Pussellawa, Nilambe, Dumbara, Rangala, Hunasgiriya, and Kotmale were in their prime. For many years the planters kept up the quality of the soil by returning to it, in the form of artificial manures, some of the essential elements. They are too poor now to make any attempts of this kind. In 1877 the value of imported manures is given in the Custom-house returns at Rs. 26,14,019. In the returns of 1881 the value is only Rs. 3,75,883. Then, again, the area over which Coffee is now grown has been greatly extended. The Brazils alone produce more than half the total amount of Coffee consumed in the world, while Ceylon scarcely ranks for one-eighteenth of that quantity; and in the Brazils, as yet, the dreaded leaf-disease has not made its appearance much felt. New fields are being opened out every day. Java and Sumatra already produce more than twice the outturn of Ceylon. India is running it very close. Coffee planting is one of the attractions in the new English venture in Borneo; and the Commissioner of British Burmah is doing all he can to make Tavoy into a Coffee district.

Altogether the planters have had a very hard time of late years. The brightest spot on their horizon is the hopes which Tea holds out to them of retrieving their fortunes. A correspondent of an Indian paper from which we have already quoted some facts says, speaking of the Ceylon planters:—

"The success of their Tea enterprise is very remarkable: one estate between Colombo and Kandy is said to have given in one year 1,000 lbs. of dry leaf to the acre. It may help your readers to appreciate this if I mention that it is found worth while to cultivate estates in the Nilgiris with so low a yield as 150 lbs., and that 400 lbs. is considered an excellent result in the north of India. What makes this outturn the more remarkable is, that the Mariawatti Estate, as it is called, is planted on land formerly occupied by Coffee, but which had been abandoned and allowed to grow into jungle. We could, unhappily, find plenty of that kind of land (hitherto supposed to be utterly valueless) in Wynaad, and as this district has been pronounced most suitable for Tea, which has done very well in one or two small plantations already existing, there are only two obstacles in our way—the want of a steady supply of labour, and the remarkable tightness of the local money market. The first difficulty has never been really grappled with, for on a Coffee estate it is usual to do but little work from March to the end of May, and the coolies are paid up and encouraged to go home during those months; but the second is a floorer. It is at once our admiration and despair to see how the Ceylon planters—with their Coffee gone, and their cinchona bark selling for twopence a-pound—go gaily on, filling new land, buying expensive machinery, and behaving generally as if they were in the most affluent circumstances."

To return to *Hemileia vastatrix*, the Coffee-leaf disease, it must be owned at once that no practical remedy has yet been found to modify its ravages. It is a minute fungus which first attacks the under sides of the leaves, causing spots or blotches, at first yellow, but subsequently turning black. These blotches are, on examination, found to be covered with a pale orange-coloured dust or powder which easily rubs off. The blotches gradually increase in size until at last they have spread over the leaves, which then drop off, leaving the tree in a short time perfectly bare, in which state they are unable to produce crop or bring to perfection the fruit they may have on them.

Carbolic acid and fumigation with sulphur and other substances have been tried, and an infinite variety of theories started to account for the origin of the spores. One correspondent writes from Batavia:—

"Regarding Coffee planting, a great deal more is talked about the leaf disease than is sanctioned by facts; the truth is that the disease was known long ago, for so far back as 1840

I was told that it was nothing new, and that it was caused by planting *dadap* between the Coffee plants for shade; and my experience since has convinced me that this is the case, for wherever Coffee is planted in forest land, or where no *dadap* trees are used for shade, there is no sign of leaf disease "—

and many other kindred "fads." High cultivation and abundance of suitable manure are all that can be recommended, with plentiful shade in the hotter localities. Very possibly a succession of wet seasons greatly tends to encourage the disease, for it should be remembered that long-continued rain washes the fertilizing matter of the soil into the subsoil and therefore away from the reach of feeding rootlets; while if a soil becomes water-logged, as it did recently on many estates, the effect is to destroy the nitrates present and evolve nitrogen as gas, thus causing a very considerable loss of plant food.

The rot shows itself—most commonly in damp, cold, upland plantations—by the young leaves and shoots of the trees turning black as though covered with soot. Hull recommends draining the ground and laying down *mana* grass two or three inches thick over the surface.

In Dominica the planters have suffered very heavily from the larva of a small moth, *Cemiostoma coffeellum*, upon which it is almost impossible to wage effective war.

In Fiji they have, especially on flats and Coffee close to the jungle, a disease called "black leaf," which is unknown in Ceylon unless "black rot" is the same. It generally comes on after several days of continuous rain, and lasts as long as the weather is at all rainy or moist, and does a great deal of damage to the foliage and crop while it lasts. The disease goes up the stem of the Coffee and along every branch in the form of a thin cobwebby string, which as soon as it reaches the leaves covers all the under surface with stuff resembling tissue paper, or say a cobweb with the meshes so close as to look like extremely fine muslin. This layer chokes the leaves and kills them effectually. The disease when in a bad form, after killing the oldest leaves, goes right into the top pair of the youngest leaves, and even kills them, leaving the bough entirely denuded of all foliage. Should it come across the berries it surrounds them with the cobweb, and dries them up, making those beans light and worthless. Should the bean happen to be ripe there is a difficulty in pulping it, and the pulper generally takes off pulp and parchment together. After the fine weather sets in the disease apparently disappears and sets in again the next rains. Fortunately Coffee planted on slopes does not suffer so much as that on flats and close to jungle; Coffee also at lower elevations than 1,000 feet escapes to a great extent.

CHAPTER XIII.

BUILDINGS AND BUNGALOWS.

THE beginner who breaks land for himself is theoretically supposed to sleep out in the open under an umbrella for the first half-year or so, until his estate is commencing to take form and shape. Really, however, there is no need for such Spartan devotion, and we cannot too strongly advise that decent and weather-proof habitations for himself and his men should be one of the planter's earliest cares. He will understand before he has been under its influence long that the Indian climate is not a thing to be played with, more particularly in districts best suited to Coffee culture. On the mountain sides, where the plants thrive, the Englishman feels alternately tropical heat and very penetrating, damp cold. Often when he turns out at five o'clock in the morning, and sips his hot Coffee, while the coolies are mustering for the day's work on the drying ground below, the forests are still dark and chill, the dew lying heavily on the low herbage; the Englishman then feeling as much affection for his log fire as he might on a November morning at home. Between eight and nine the estate and woods are pleasant enough; at ten they are often "roasting" hot, and so they continue until the sun goes down once more, and Nature refreshes itself in the cool of the evening.

When a wet monsoon is raging in Ceylon or India, the rain descends in blinding torrents, none but the stoutest and best-made roofs withstanding it. The estate bungalow should be just under the crest of a commanding hillock, as near the centre of the estate as possible. The main road should run close by if possible, while the coolie lines should lie within sight, but not too close, and the stores and pulping houses also handy. If the bungalow hill is two hundred feet or so above the surrounding country, it will probably get whatever breezes there are blowing in the hot weather, and will be healthier. The view also should be good—no mean consideration after a hard day's work to a lonely man.

To right and left, perhaps, the high mountains shut off the quarter of each monsoon, and looking southward down the winding valley, the eye ranges over long expanses of unclaimed jungle stretching right away to the grey distance—a wilderness, the home of the bison and elephant, all "impenetrable jungle." To the north we look along the course of the road, which leads over half-a-dozen estates, buried in deep frames of jungle, each with its little white bungalow and dusky coolie "lines;" and amid most one catches here and there the flashing of a pool or streamlet, the all-important water for turning the pulping machinery and supplying the coolies. Farther away the ghaut road begins, and, the hills sloping down, nothing more is seen of the forest until the lowlands unrol themselves, stretching far away like a wonderful fabric of green and grey cloth. At this distance towns and villages cannot be made out, but just where the great fertile plain melts away into indistinguishable distance, again towering mountains rise up, ascending tier above tier into the sky. Such a view, we cannot but think, may do much to keep a man healthful and contented.

This house, however, is not put up directly. The planter, when he has purchased land and has to open it, generally manages to get a " shake down " for the first month or so at the bungalow of some neighbour, paying him, of course, for board and lodging, and walking to and fro between the new and old estate every day; the coolies doing the same and billeting themselves as they best may, unless there are villages at hand, upon the natives of the established estate. After a little while of this, an Englishman will probably be glad enough to set up housekeeping for himself. The first rough bungalow should be built close by the site of the future substantial erection, so that advantages of pure air, water, &c., may be obtained at once, a vegetable garden formed on the hill top, and so on. The first hut often comes in afterwards as a kitchen. Its construction is primitive, and not above the capacities of intelligent carpenter coolies, of whom there are generally some at hand ready to turn to this work for wages a trifle higher than those of the ordinary labourer. Four posts at the corners of a space, say, 14 feet by 20 feet are sunk firmly into the ground and connected along the tops by long, light poles. Strong pillars at either end serve to take the sapling which forms the ridge of the roof. Stakes are driven in all round the sides and lashed along the roof framework until the half-finished hut bears a close resemblance to a gigantic birdcage. "Palghaut mats," made of closely woven split rattan cane, are then laced along the outside and inside as *walls*, and a thick thatch of palm leaves or jungle grass makes a good roof.

Every planter remembers his first hut in the jungle, even cherishing an affection for it long after wind and rain have reduced it to its original elements. In my own primitive hut the roof, extra thick, with the eaves brought to within four feet of the ground to protect the sides, was made of the long sweet-scented lemon-grass, and there were three little glass windows, a door with a rough porch, and a wall of matting across the interior to divide the sleeping compartment from the day-room. Altogether it was a strange little place, pretty to look at while the materials were fresh and clean, but not good for hard use—the daylight streaming through the two thicknesses of matting in many places, and the wind coming in at every corner;

while after a shower every part got damp, and, being entirely built of vegetable produce, there was a very strong odour of decaying matter—something between wet hay and bilge-water on a steamer. When dry, the lemon-grass had it all its own way, and the scent then was very pleasant.

A little "roughing it" must be expected and put up with at this time, the most important matters being to secure a healthy spot with command of good water, protection from the night dews and chills—to keep out the damp of an Indian monsoon is more than any house built by human hands can be expected to achieve.

A boarded floor, however, a foot clear above the ground, is an important sanitary feature which should never be overlooked. If the doors and windows of the permanent bungalow are got up from the agents about this time they will do duty for a period in the humbler structure.

The natives house themselves temporarily in "lines"—*i.e.*, long, low sheds with matting sides, thatch roofs, and beaten mud floors. There must be running water near, but not close enough to receive the refuse of the huts which heavy rains will wash down. With proper guidance, and when they feel the authority of a strong hand, the coolies may be trained to any point of order and discipline. Left to themselves, the lower classes, who are swept together by the maistries in the lowlands and brought up on the advance system, are unquestionably careless and objectionable in domestic arrangements. Their huts and the surrounding paths and Coffee will get into a hopelessly filthy condition unless sanitary measures are introduced early. It is a good plan to employ a couple of low-caste coolies on special wages to go round daily with mammoties and attend to these matters.

When the Coffee is planted, and before the trees come into bearing, it is time to prepare and consider the plans of permanent and substantial buildings. These may be either of

   (1) Stone and mortar,
   (2) Bricks and mortar,
   (3) Bricks or stone with mud,
   (4) Wattle and daub,
   (5) Laterite and mortar,
   (6) Wooden boards or logs.

Iron-roofed houses might, perhaps, be included, but they have many and manifold objections, and cannot be recommended except for stores and pulping sheds. One planter declares in favour of sun-dried bricks with good mortar. " They give sufficient strength, are easily transported and used, and above all are cheap, being made almost anywhere. A common mason will lay from 400 to 500 large-sized (say 7 lb.) bricks per day; eight of these will just make up an ordinary coolie load, and their dimensions will probably be about $10\frac{1}{2}$ by $5\frac{1}{4}$ by $3\frac{1}{2}$

inches. The earth best suited for the manufacture of bricks should contain a mixture of about five parts of pure clay to one of sand. Almost any kind of earth will do more or less well, provided it is free from pebbles and not too sandy."

To make good bricks, however, is a science in itself which cannot be taught in a paragraph. The top strata of vegetable earth is removed from the ground intended to be used as material, and the subsoil is then flooded with water and worked up by the feet of cattle or elephants into the consistency of dough. It is next pressed into damped wooden moulds, and slipped out of them to dry on a previously levelled space, where the bricks must be protected from sun and wind. They are built up with abundance of firewood to be fired into clumps six or seven feet high, a week being devoted to burning, and another allowed during which they are cooling.

A brick-built house is comfortable and substantial, but it is not a practical possibility in every district, owing to the care and skilled labour required. Bungalows built of weather-boarding are the commonest for a variety of reasons. Not the least important of these lies in the fact that every native village has a professional carpenter and his "hands," who are quite capable of satisfying the planter's first needs in this direction; and a word from the estate's local native agent in the plains will send them trooping up to the jungle, on pay or on contract, with all their curious but effective tools, and ready to undertake any amount of simple house-building operations they may be set to. Then, again, there often seems but little inducement to manufacture bricks or prepare wattle and daub when abundance of noble timber lies seasoning in the clearings—suggesting planks enough to build an Armada!

If the risk of fire—the chief objection to be urged against wood—is accepted, the first thing to be done is to send for a gang of professional sawyers. These men live by this work; they are honest and trustworthy, since it will readily be understood that double-dealings regarding pay, &c., would lead to the gang obtaining a bad name, and consequent loss of patronage.

Hall says the professional sawyers of Southern India have caste objections to any work other than actual sawing. He found they would not even move logs into place for their own use, requiring this to be done by the estate coolies. Those who worked for me never raised any objections of this kind. They heard the manner and quantity of timber required—so much planking, so many posts, rafters, &c.—and then, selecting a suitable trunk in one of the clearings, built an open platform of strong uprights and reliable baulks on the *lower* side, afterwards rolling the log lengthways on to it.

While this work is going on and the piles of red cedar planks, or orange-yellow jack "framings"

BUILDINGS AND BUNGALOWS.   143

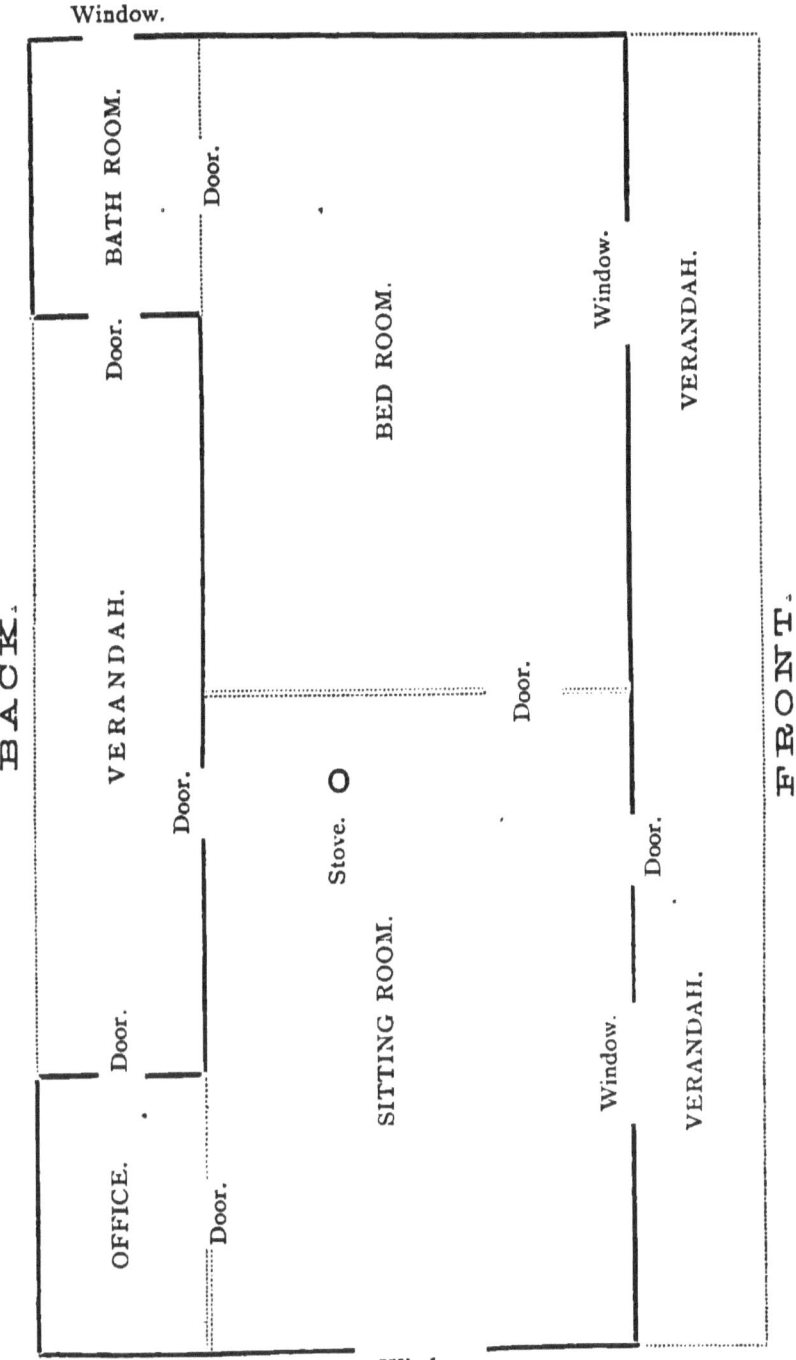

and door posts are growing, plans of the future house, as also the spot for it, have to be prepared. The accompanying ground plan of an Assistant Superintendent's bungalow, or one quite sufficient for the needs of a private estate until it has grown prosperous and extensive, will give an idea of the kind of lodge usually built.

The two main rooms are used as a sleeping room and as a living room. Out of the former is a bath room, with its big wooden tub occupying the centre, while adjoining the latter is an "office" where estàte books are kept, and the medicine chest is situated. A good verandah front and back adds greatly to comfort and appearance of the house—a verandahless bungalow in the long and stormy rainy season is a misery. A guest room can be added on to the above little domicile with little extra expense. The "boys'" house and kitchen will be behind, and a covered path should lead into the back verandah from them. Halfway down the hill are stables, and beyond the coolie lines, and on the side of the bungalow facing these, hangs the gong or bell wherewith the "chick doree" rouses the coolies at five in the morning, and calls them back from work at six p.m.

Wattle and daub are favourite materials, almost as good as brick and mortar. The corner pieces, doorposts, and main uprights forming sides of a house of this kind should be of squared timber, and of some species such as "kino" or black wood, teak or *Pterocarpus marsupium*, not liable to shrink, warp, or be destroyed by the ever-present white ants. As far as the latter go, however, no wood is absolutely safe against their persistent efforts. Something may be done by charring ends of beams, steeping them in creosote, tar, or kerosene, the latter strongly recommended; but after all these precautions, ants will still find their way into the wood, and increase and multiply. It does not follow that, when they have entered, a house is henceforth unsafe or uninhabitable by human tenants. Neither termites nor rats will willingly endanger the place of their residence. Though rats have swarmed on board ships probably since commerce began, no case is known in which they have sunk a vessel by deliberately letting the sea through her sides. In the same way white ants, though they fill beams with passages, instinctively leave enough wood to ensure the support doing its duty. The kneaded clay of a "wattle and daub" house is in itself very strong after the sun-scorching of a hot season. In constructing it, the squared corner pieces, having been gone over with preservative liquid, are sunk a couple of feet or more in the ground. Other posts, similar to these, embedded equally deep, should come at four or five feet apart, and between each pair, again, a couple of other uprights, that need not, perhaps, be sawn or buried deeply in the soil. There will thus be spaces of about a foot between the supports. Across these, laths or split bamboo are nailed horizontally, and into the hollow wall thus built up, worked clay, the same as that used for preparing bricks, is firmly trodden in, stones being occasionally added and rammed down to send the "daub" into all cracks and corners.

When our walls are dry, they may have another coating of clay inside and out, covering all the woodwork, and bringing their thickness up to ten inches or a foot; and finally an inside service of "chunam," *i.e.*, plaster, and a harling of whitewash will make them neat and inhabitable. Buildings of this sort will last for forty or fifty years—that is to say, as long as the Coffee itself.

"Cabook" or "laterite" is a kind of decomposed rock which has the convenient faculty of becoming hard by exposure to the atmosphere. It is cut out some six to ten feet below the surface in blocks or bricks about 15 in. in length by 9 in. by 6 in., with an axe or spade; these bricks becoming hard in a few days make neat as well as substantial walls.

Perhaps wattle and mud is as good as anything for coolie lines. It is much the same as they have always been accustomed to; it is fireproof, and not expensive. Both inside and outside should be kept perfectly smooth with plaster, and gone over occasionally with chunam to keep down insects.

Eight or ten rooms side by side and under one roof is as many as it is advisable to put together. Each family owns a room, and the castes are less likely to interfere with one another's comfort when the dwelling spaces are in limited blocks.

As many sets of lines must be built as there are coolies to be housed. The position of these huts must be selected with forethought (taking care to remember fever mists collect in hollows, where very likely natives would prefer to lodge themselves); but, on the other hand, they cannot appreciate or stand the bracing air of the elevated hillside which Englishmen naturally select.

Their "lines" should abut on some waste grass land, if possible, in order that live stock may be kept without danger to the Coffee, and gardens started by the coolies so inclined.

Water should be abundant and pure. This is a consideration of the first importance. Good fresh air and plenty of it is desirable. Never put "lines" close up to a bank or rock; let there be space for air and cleaning all round. And, lastly, there is the item of dryness of the houses themselves to be secured by making the walls substantial—the eaves coming down rather low, thus forming a good broad verandah along the front, and by raising the floor one or two feet above the ground level. There are neither windows nor chimneys in these rooms, but each should have a substantial well-hinged door (2 feet 6 inches will be wide enough) of its own. Fires are lit in one corner, and smoke finds its own way out through roof or doorway as it likes. Strong wooden benches should run half round the room for the inmates to sleep on—never let them lie on the ground. In some Coffee districts the housing of the labourers is a matter for Government inspection; and it is always good, sound policy to make the workers contented and comfortable.

Pulping and drying sheds are alluded to in the succeeding chapters, here it is not necessary to go very fully into their construction, since they are amongst the last requirements of the estate. Before they have to be put up, the planter will probably have been round his district and learnt by personal inspection the peculiar designs of the country, the forms best suited to its needs, and last, but not least, to what style the length of his purse justifies him in going.

Cattle sheds, tool sheds, stables, and storehouses will have to be erected from time to time. Their cost and build will vary considerably according to the material selected for their construction, and whether the locality is advanced in civilization or only partially opened jungle.

Perhaps the most important item in all buildings is the roof, and special care should be given to it. Iron roofing is only suitable to pulping sheds and stores. The sheets are not nailed down, as they might be in England, but buckled together with iron Z's. Palm leaf roofs are picturesque and well enough, but dangerous and not permanent; lemon-grass thatching always leaks like a sieve under its first "drencher," but improves as it felts down to a compact mass. Shingles, or "slates" split from a straight-fibred tree, are very widely used. But "not one-half the persons who lay shingles have a correct idea of making a roof that will be absolutely rain-tight during a driving storm," says the *Canadian Mechanic*. The correct rule for laying shingles of any length, in order to form a roof leak-tight, is to lay the courses less than one-third the length of the shortest shingles. For example, when shingles are 18 inches long, many of them will not be more than 17 inches in length; therefore 5 inches is all that the course will bear to be laid to the weather with surety of forming a good roof. The shingles must be three thicknesses over the entire roof. If they are not three thicknesses —if now and then a shingle lacks a quarter or half an inch of being long enough to make three thicknesses—there will in all probability be a leaky place in the roof at such a point. Moreover, when the lower courses lack half-an-inch of extending up far enough to receive the rain from the outermost course, in case the middle course were removed, it would be just as well to lay them 7 inches or 8 inches to the weather as to lay them only 5 inches or 5½ inches. Many shingles are only 16 inches long, and many that are sold for 16 inches long will hardly measure 15 inches. In this case— if the roof be rather flat, say about one quarter pitch—4½ inches is as far as they should be laid to the weather. In case a roof were quite steep, it might answer to lay the courses 4¾ inches to the weather. When buildings are erected by the job, proprietors should give their personal attention to this subject, and see that jobbers do not lay the courses a half-inch too far to the weather.

Shingles boiled for half-an-hour in a solution of lime and salt, which penetrates every particle of the wood, are rendered, in a large measure, fireproof and their durability greatly increased. Tiles are admirable but expensive.

Estate buildings give infinite scope to the vanity or the carelessness of responsible authorities. While a reckless outlay is ruinous to a young estate, we strongly hold the opinion that every foot of covered space (when once the temporary shelters are put aside) should be substantial and serviceable. Between £1,500 and £2,000 is usually considered to be the amount for which an estate of 200 acres can be thoroughly established in every necessary permanent building. For from Rs. 700 to 1,000, according to locality, &c., a small bungalow of wattle and daub, or weather boarded, with shingle roof and galvanized iron spouting, can be put up, consisting of dining room, two bedrooms, office, bath-house, &c., and the whole raised on stone pillars a few feet above the ground.

A first-class bungalow for a married Englishman and family would cost something like Rs. 5,000. Elliot, who wrote at a time when everything was cheaper than it is now, thinks something might be done in the way of a temporary habitation for Rs. 350, and suggests it is better to spend that sum only until the success of the estate is assured than to sink as many pounds at the beginning. On a new estate, where timber was plentiful, we could build for Rs. 3,500 a very superior house, with two living rooms, five bedrooms, office and bath-rooms, kitchen and servants' rooms, stables for two horses, &c., &c., all on a raised stone foundation.

Furniture and furnishing are items that must not be overlooked.

Lines.—Twenty rooms, roof and walls of cadjans or talipots, can be erected at a cost of Rs. 10 a room (site included), which will be watertight and comfortable, and last for all the time they are wanted; they can be run up in a few days—a great consideration—and there is no risk of the coolies catching illness from wet mud walls and damp floors. A line of this sort should accommodate 100 labourers. A shallow drain should be cut *all round* the line to keep the floors dry. A permanent set of rooms can be built at leisure. For a 200-acre estate we might thus say temporary lines would cost Rs. 200, and permanent lines Rs. 300. More lines would be needed afterwards perhaps.

Under the head of bungalows and lines, Mr. Sabonadière argues strongly for permanent buildings of stone with shingled roofs.

Store.—Stone pillars, roof of galvanised Morewood's tiles, sawn timber, coir-matting floors in three storeys, £485.

Pulping House.—Solid masonry, pillars, and cisterns; a double floor for curing purposes, corrugated iron roof, but not including cost of machinery, £483.

Bungalow.—Outside walls of stone, inner walls, sawn timber, mudded between sawn reapers, planked floors, and shingle roof, and including £70 as cost of godowns, £356.

These are his estimates, and they represent the very best class of buildings. For £200 (Rs. 2,000) it would be possible to build a very decent pulping shed and store-house, 20 ft. by 10 ft. and 40 ft. by 20 ft., of sawn timber and iron roofed, with cherry lofts sufficient for all the requirements of a first and second crop.

All these erections are so expensive and important that the young planter should not be in a hurry to build, but should rather make a study of those successfully working in his district, and carefully watch the wants and peculiarities of his own estate before beginning.

CHAPTER XIV.

ROADING AND DRAINING.

THE presiding government is bound to make and keep in repair the main thoroughfares of every territory, usually levying a tax for the purpose; but the planter has to make his own local roadways. The cheapest is what we call a dug-out road; that is to say, the hillside being very steep, soil is shovelled away from the upper part and placed on the lower side till the road comes level. Thus there is a perpendicular wall on one hand and a steep scarp on the other, and being smoothed, the fresh black earth looks neat and nice, but requires some time to settle down. At first, owing to half the breadth being cut out of the solid, and half composed of loose soil, it is apt to sink on the outer side, and has to be repaired. Cutting through fallen logs and rolling them away is a source of chief expense. On the hillside the great stems will usually lie as they have fallen, up and down the slope, sometimes two or three deep; and as the road runs along parallel with the valley, it meets them all at right angles. Since they are far beyond the planter's power to move, even after the best of burns as they lie, he has to cut through them at all costs. Charred stumps are almost worse than the fallen stems. Elsewhere I have mentioned amongst my earliest road-making experiences how now and again it was the stump of one of these forest giants, that had been cut off five feet above the ground, which we had to draw, like a mighty tooth. One or two of these stumps took us perhaps four or five days' toil. The first day's would go in scratching away soil and undermining roots, and when those were laid bare we had the task of cutting through them, many being underground branches as thick as the stem of a small tree. When at last they were severed, all available hands mustered, and, with crowbars and long levers, the stump was slowly hoisted out amongst frantic cries of maistries and shouts of perspiring coolies, to be rolled down the hillside, there to stay for twenty or thirty years, until sun and rain have resolved it into dust. The greater proportion of the trees were cut through in two places, and the intermediate portion was rolled away easily enough; but sometimes, in spite of my utmost engineering skill, the upper portion of the trunk would come rolling down the hill-slope, sending everyone flying for life, and blocking up the track again.

Gradients should be as slight as possible, and all roads well planned and thought of beforehand. They should centre at the superintendent's bungalow or at the stores. It is better to have them on ridges than in valleys, but halfway between crest and bottom is the proper line for them to take.

Though "dug-outs" are, as we have said, the cheapest, yet it is better and more "pucka" to dig a road from the solid, going, say, one foot deep on the level. On both sides there should then be good 18 in. by 18 in. drains, with occasional culverts across the road covered in by logs or stones.

Metalling is rarely attempted on these private thoroughfares, and the same may be said of bridges. If a bridge *must* be made it is usually constructed of logs placed side by side, resting on broad stone buttresses. We have traced a good many miles of road with a surveyor's level and compass, but with a little training the eye becomes sufficiently accurate, and stumps can be "dodged," and fords much more conveniently approached by the latter means than when instruments are used. "He who traces, clears, and partially cuts his roads at the earliest possible time will save five per cent. on all the work he has to do in the field." A mile of road to every twenty or thirty acres is little too much. These roads may be made narrow at first, and afterwards (when the estate needs cart traffic) widened out to ten or twelve feet. But if they are left untraced and not begun until after planting is over, there will be a reluctance to destroy flourishing bushes, and roads will hardly be so wide or so numerous as they should; 1 in 15, 1 in 20, 1 in 25 are fair gradients for an estate not very full of rocks and nullahs. Care should he taken that the road is not liable to be flooded by a sudden rise in a stream or torrent—*i.e.*, when the track has crossed a ravine do not let it slope uniformly downwards, thus tempting the next spate to take a new course along your dug-out, but let there be a gentle rise of five or six feet, and then you can go on with your descending gradient again.

Two men will cut one average chain of road per day, one foot into the solid sloping *inwards* to the drain, and clear everything off excepting heavier stuff. In light, standing jungle the path will move forward with wonderful rapidity: in clearings as pointed out it is a very different matter. Rs. 150 per mile may, however, be taken as an average cost, mounting to Rs. 250 and 300 in heavy prostrate timber or rocky land. Dynamite and gunpowder sometimes expedite the removal of troublesome stumps, &c.

Draining is a kindred occupation, which should be done if possible before the first wet season, and at the same time with the roads. Drains are usually half a chain apart, and falling to the nearest nullah by a gradient of 1 in 18 or 1 in 15. According to the steepness of the land so must the size and frequency of channels be (taking a drain of 2 feet wide, and 18 inches deep, as an average), and the further the water has to run to an outflow the broader the drain should be made. The purpose of this work is that when a deluge of tropical rain descends it shall be intercepted, and led off the land before a head is gathered, and a muddy yellow sheet of water scours down the hillside, taking tons of soil with it. "Water holes" and terracing have been tried, but "no one has ever made holes big enough, or embankments strong enough, to meet the requirements of the case. All precautions may be taken, with satisfactory results for a long time; yet the day comes when all is of no avail: embankments give way, holes overflow, the water gathers body and force, and rushes down the hill sweeping away every obstacle, leaving a deep trench behind it down to the subsoil, and often far into it, all which may be the work of a few minutes, and thus the labour and watching of years is neutralized in an hour."

Good drains of average size and half a chain apart are cut at the rate of about Rs. 10 per acre. The upkeep of roads and drains—that is to say, the regular clearing of them out and repairing—amounts to between Rs. 2 and 3, according to the care and skill with which they were originally constructed.

CHAPTER XV.

THE CROP.

It is not until the third year that any real recompense comes for the long and tedious labour bestowed upon the preparation of the estate, but at the end of that time a reward is at hand. About the beginning of the new year, early in January, the planter will notice his bushes covered with clusters of small, hard, green buds, springing, seven or eight together, from the junction of the leaves and branches. These are the future flowers which have to repay all the trouble and expense incurred. As time goes on they ripen and swell rapidly, turning from opaque green to cream and yellow-white, until one morning in March, or perhaps April if the situation is wet and cold, the first "flush" is out. Far and near, as we described in a first chapter, the undulations of garden are bathed in a fascinating sea of white blossoms; near at hand the starlike flowers glisten amongst glossy masses of leafage, clear in every detail, while further away the long rows of bushes are crested with a confused streak of white like many rows of breakers on a shallow shore. Every individual blossom somewhat resembles that of an orange, and from great masses of them grown together a very powerful odour is given forth, which, if not quite so pleasant as that of the golden fruit, is powerful and sweet. This scent is said to bring on feverish symptoms, but we should rather be inclined to believe that the blossoming season—always a feverish time—more than the flowers themselves, was to blame. A hot morning after rain brings out bloom upon the bushes, and (though it must be said with regret) brings out that miasma from the decayed vegetation so much dreaded by the planter. Rain at this time is hurtful to the prospects of a large crop. When it falls upon the flowers the pistils in the centre subsequently show a black speck, and the cherry that should follow never comes to anything.

For the purpose of illustrating the system of rainfall of Southern India, the year may be conveniently divided into two equal periods—viz., from the 1st October to the 31st March, and from the 1st April to the 30th September—the bulk of the rainfall in these periods being due to the south-west and north-east monsoon respectively. The south-west monsoon commences to blow in the end of May or beginning of June, and a great portion of the vapour brought with it from the Indian Ocean is intercepted and condensed by the Western Ghâts, and precipitated in torrents of rain on the strip of land between these mountains and the sea, which forms the district of Malabar and Canara, and the kingdoms of Travancore and Cochin. A portion, however, passes over the range, or through the gaps which here and there occur, and finds its way in more or less abundance to every district in the Presidency. The minor showers of April are not due to the influence of either monsoon, yet it is just the light "sprinklings" which make all the difference, to Travancore Coffee at any rate. Coming before their time they do immense mischief, but in season when fruit has "set," *i.e.*, fructification been accomplished, they knock off the withered brown petals and afford the plants much service by watering them at a period when all possible encouragement is needed. Coffee for this reason is a very precarious investment in Travancore. The crop is entirely dependent upon rain after the blossoming season, a few showers just at the right time making a difference of thousands of rupees to the planter. As soon as the flowers are off, the little green nobs at the bottom begin to swell, filling out rapidly all the hot weather, changing colour early in the autumn from green to yellow, and about October assuming the red tinge which marks approaching ripeness.

According to the season this will be earlier or later, while different corners of the estate will ripen at various times according as the land has a warm or cold aspect—even opposite sides of a bush often vary considerably in this respect. A good watch must be kept for the first berries ready, and it is as well to turn pickers—a few at first—into the clearings directly there is anything worth their picking, since, if the crop is a good one, and allowed to ripen throughout on the bushes, very few estates are so well supplied with labour as to be ready to properly strip the bushes before much cherry has followed its natural destination and fallen overripe to the ground, or vanished under attacks of birds and animals. So we begin at once, in order to keep pace with the ripening berries, and usually three, or at the most four, gleanings—the middle pick being always the most considerable—lasting from November to January, will be sufficient to store all there is to be had that season.

Men, women, and children are employed at the picking season, and it is a sight lively enough to see them marshalled along the head of a clearing in the early morning waiting for the signal to begin, while white-clad maistries run hither and thither brandishing their sticks and seeing each row of Coffee has its picker, so that every tree may be fairly searched. As we noticed under "Weeding," the active and delicate fingers of women or children rival at this task those of the men. All being paid *pro rata*, it is a good time for the coolies, who, on an estate which they like, are unusually industrious and jovial at "cherry ripe" season.

Each worker carries a bag slung from his or her shoulder, into which they stuff the coloured berries with both hands as fast as picked. When the wallet is full it is taken to the nearest roadway, where stand the coolies' rows of receiving sacks, each capable of holding a bushel or two bushels of fruit. By the number of these journeys the workers estimate the quantity they have picked, and mentally feel the pay in rupees growing heavy in their cummerbunds. If there is plenty of crop, each picker should collect three or perhaps three-and-a-half bushels a-day, for which the pay is the equivalent of fourpence per bushel.

As the big sacks are filled, they are taken off to the pulping sheds, and should be, if it can possibly be managed, operated upon within a few hours, or certainly the same day, as any delay may cause the heaps of soft ripe fruit to ferment, discolouring the inside parchment and depreciating the value of the sample in Mincing Lane. It is, however, not invariably the rule to pulp at once. In Brazil, much of the Coffee is purposely allowed to stand in sheds for forty-eight hours, thereby attaining a peculiar odour that recommends it to South American connoisseurs. Again, native and Dutch Coffee is not pulped but *hulled;* instead of the soft outside covering of flesh being removed by pulping machinery, it is suffered to dry upon the beans, and is subsequently operated upon by special machinery which cracks off this dried husk.

THE CROP.

The riper the fruit is upon the trees before it is gathered, the better will be the resulting sample of prepared Coffee. The observant Arabs spread mats under their world-famous Mocha bushes, and collect only those cherries falling into them when the tree is shaken. But the European planter can hardly follow this process, because, as we have said, his command of labour is hardly sufficient even to gather in the heavy crops his system of planting brings about in the quickest and most expeditious of ways.

Anything tending to economise labour at this season is of high value. There is a method by which "cherries" are sent down from the most remote clearings by means of water power. This is done by iron piping, about the same diameter and strength as the familiar cast-iron conducts "adorning" the outside of English houses. Six or eight foot lengths of this tubing are put together after starting from some convenient and central spot on the estate where a fair flow of water can always be obtained, though it need not be more than a rivulet, and length after length it is wound down the estate to the pulping house. Some care and skill is required in erecting them. Where streams and ravines are crossed the pipes must be supported on trestles, and where they lie along the ground, firmly pegged down. At the receiving stations are coolies who receive the cherry and flood it down the tube with sufficient water, so much at a time, and thus it goes by steady gradient and regular curves into the cisterns of the curing room. Large as the prime cost of this spouting undoubtedly is (£300 should furnish a 200-acre plantation), on extensive estates it cannot fail to pay. "The coolies are able to gather a larger quantity, and they are saved bodily wear and tear. With a force of 200 coolies in the field, an increase of at least 100 bushels, or 10 cwts. a-day, may be safely reckoned upon, amouting say to 300 cwts. for the five heavy weeks of picking, and representing a money value of fully £1,002 in the London market," calculates Mr. Sabonadiere!

We have said real returns for labour and capital invested in a Coffee estate only begin in the third year. This statement must be modified to the extent of acknowledging there is sometimes a maiden crop, a slight one generally, though in very good soil and in a dry climate as much as from seven to nine cwt. per acre has been got as first fruits in a second year. This, needless to say, must be picked as it comes ripe; and if pulping machinery is not yet up on the estate, it may be sold in bulk to some neighbouring, better established planter. 1 lb. per tree is a very paying quantity of Coffee all over an estate; but as much as 2 lbs. or even 3 lbs. are sometimes got, and 5 cwt. per acre is a satisfactory average, though those estates making their happy possessor's fortunes give far more. The Rothschild estate of Ceylon, for instance, from 1865 to 1871 returned 9½ cwt. per acre. One-third of this estate was on Patna soil.

When coolies do not receive tallies, to be redeemed on the following pay day, or cash—*kai kasi* they call it—for the weight of cherry brought in and weighed in the cherry loft of the pulping shed, the planter sets them a daily task—one and a-half bushels, one bushel, three-quarters, or even one-third of a bushel, according to the state of the crop. Hands at this season should never be paid by this ordinary daily wage, which holds out no encouragement to extra exertions.

Always, when possible, let work begin on the highest ground, or amongst those bushes furthest from the roads; and thus, as day declines and the men are tired, journeys will be shorter and there will be but few wearisome climbs with an empty cooty sack to finish off a half-dozen bushes perhaps. Fallen berries, of course, are picked up, and, to tell the truth, make by far the best-flavoured Coffee.

There is some danger in paying coolies in full as they earn their money; the danger is that they will go away to the nearest bazaar in the middle of this busiest season and waste their substance in riotous living, regardless of their master's pressing needs. It is better to make it a rule to advance only an anna or two each evening—sufficient to be cheerful but not uproarious upon.

The only other thing to be said is, that four or six annas per bushel, according to the scarcity of labour, &c., is the usual price paid; other expenses come more regularly under the next heading.

CHAPTER XVI.

PULPING AND PREPARING.

The final curing of the Coffee bean, the freeing from all outside pulp and coverings, in order that it may go to market in the form which an English public is familiar with, is a matter of importance. Briefly summarised, the processes are these:—

The cherry is passed through the pulper, and the pulp, or skin, is pulled off, leaving the parchment bean all covered with saccharine matter, so much so that it is impossible to grasp a handful of it and retain it all. It is to remove this that fermentation is allowed. After fermentation, the Coffee is washed; it then presents the appearance of a bean covered with a strong white skin, or husk, called parchment. This is exposed for several days to a strong sun, and, when dry enough, is packed off, say to Colombo. Here it is again dried for two to three days, and then husked by being put into a circular trough, over which roll four or two enormous wheels, weighing generally a ton each. These remove the husk without injuring the bean, and now the bean presents a changed appearance; it is closely fitted with a thin skin of silver, called the silver skin. This is winnowed off, and the Coffee packed for sale. Should the Coffee be allowed to ferment too long, it will give the husk a black appearance instead of the snowy white one it should have; and, although this does not injure the inner contents, the brokers will depreciate its value. Besides all this, the beans are very carefully graded and sifted into sizes, as a regular sample makes a considerable difference in price obtained.

Some Coffee is not pulped but "hulled," and chiefly that grown in the Dutch Islands and some States of South America. The hulling process consists of drying the cherries just as they come in from the fields—withering them, perhaps, would better express it — and afterwards cracking off the husk by submitting it to pressure under two heavy wheels running round in a circular trough.

If the planter has erected no buildings of his own when his early crops come to hand, this hulling is the only plan for him to follow. He spreads out the stores of red cherries on a previously prepared drying ground covered with mats, and, keeping them moved with rakes or by the feet of coolies, extracts all moisture. Subsequently the withered fruit is done up in strong bags and sent down to the "Agents" on the coast, who "hull" it in their own machinery, or at least know where to get it done.

PULPING AND PREPARING. 169

The annexed illustration represents one of Messrs. Gordon's "Improved Peeling or Hulling Mills," and will give a novice an idea of the sort of machinery used. A "circular" of that firm,

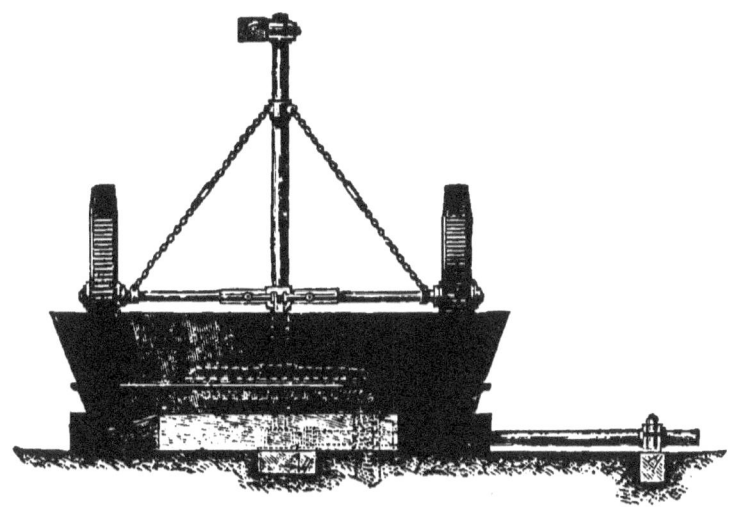

IMPROVED PEELING OR HULLING MILL.

(which holds the first place in the manufacture of all mechanical contrivances demanded by the modern Coffee planter) says:—

"From repeated experiments and trials, we are convinced that for effectually and quickly peeling and polishing the Coffee bean without breakage, nothing excels this machine. It will clean Coffee dried either in the cherry or in the parchment. The machine is simple both in construction and in working, durable, and not liable to break down. With the same power it will clean a larger quantity than most other machines. J. Gordon and Co. have themselves frequently seen 2,400 lbs. peeled per hour with one of these mills, and with little or no breakage, while a badly constructed mill will break as much as it will clean."

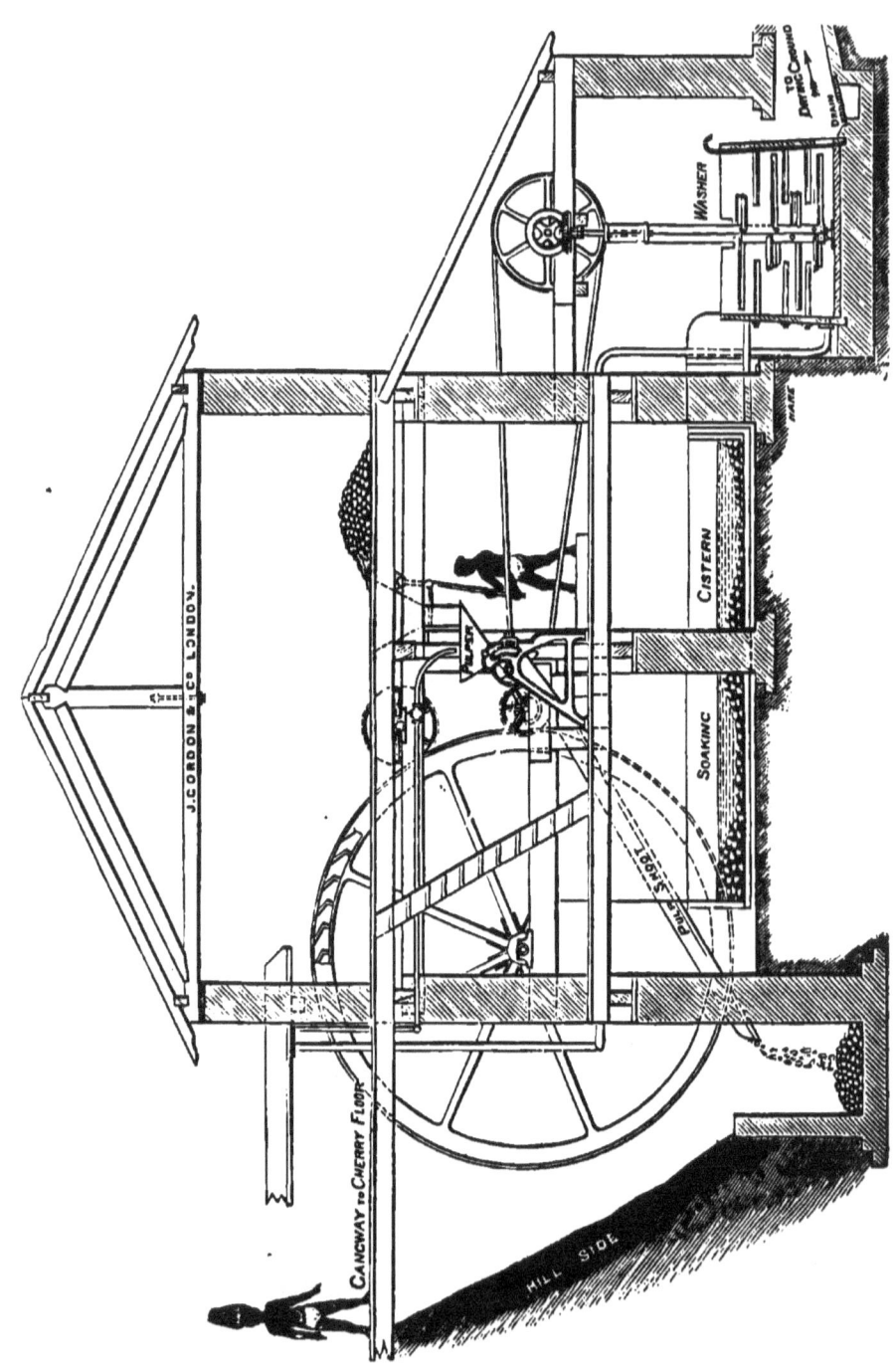

PULPING AND PREPARING. 171

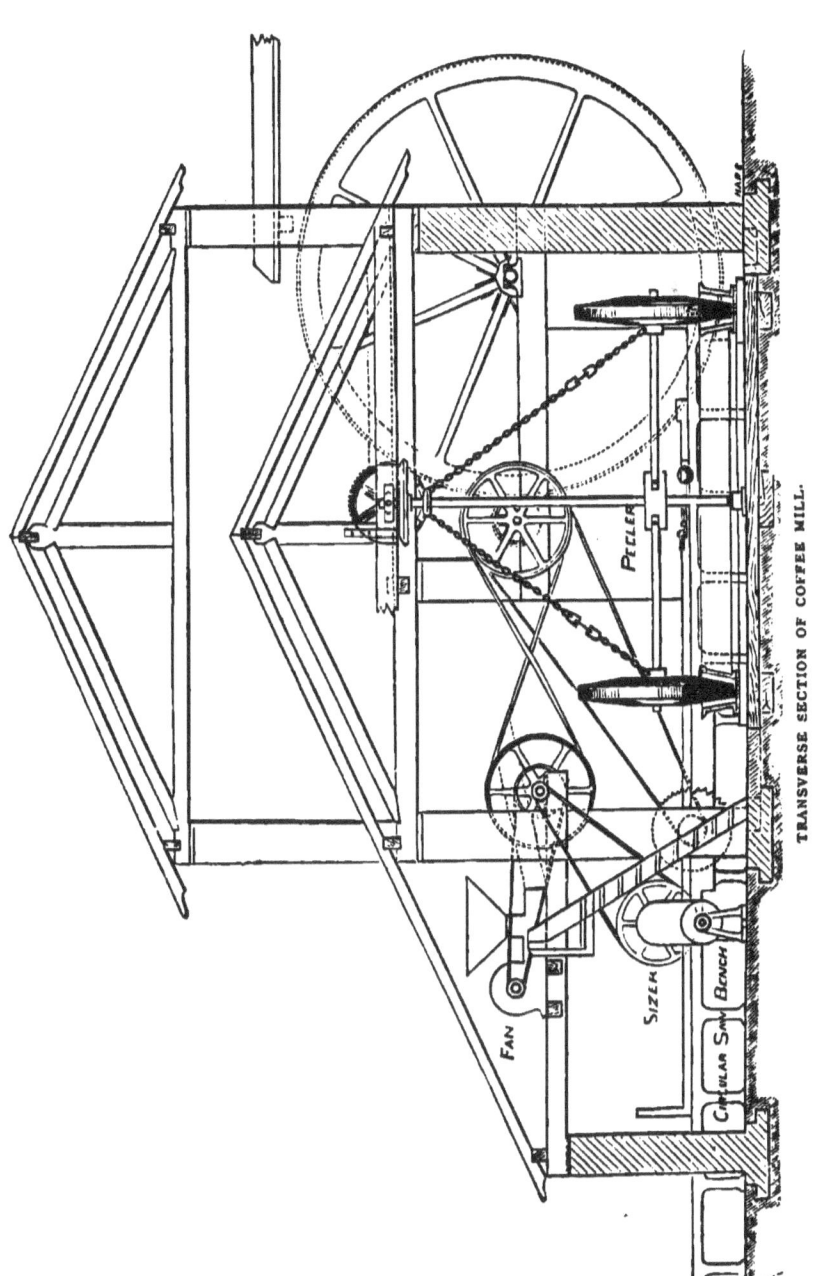

TRANSVERSE SECTION OF COFFEE MILL.

It may be as well, perhaps, to add the prices, which are:—

Diameter-centre of Wheel.	Quantity Cleaned per Hour.	Price.
14 feet.	2,400 lbs.	£140
12 ,,	1,800 ,,	£110
10 ,,	1,400 ,,	£96
9 ,,	1,200 ,,	£88
7 ,,	800 ,,	£70

If, however, the estate is large and forward enough —a "company estate," for instance, of a thousand or two of acres—to demand its own private buildings, and mills for pulping, drying, sorting, &c., then elaborate machinery has to be established. It is not possible here to go into technical architectural details of the buildings required, but Messrs. Gordon having kindly supplied us with particulars of the latest and most approved forms of pulping sheds, we give the accompanying outlines, feeling sure that a diagram will convey a much clearer impression than many pages of print.

Here it will be seen, to begin with, that cherry arrives on the head of a coolie entering the loft by a level gangway instead of having to toil up a ladder or steps, who puts down his load where it can conveniently be sent below to the pulper, taking his brass cheque for quantity delivered in return. Towards this end these buildings are usually placed against a rock face or dug-away embankment, which brings their roof nearly flush with the upper surface of the ground, and materially lightens the labour of bringing in crop.

Of course, with a complete service of iron delivery spouting, the top floor entry is not so essential; but even then it is as well to have it

"DISC" PULPER.

in case anything goes wrong with your alternate method, and you have to fall back upon coolie carriage. From the cherry floor the ripe berries just picked go down into the "pulper," where a man is stationed to regulate the quantity admitted. The pulper is just a gigantic revolving nutmeg grater. The principle of the machine is that the pulp of the Coffee is partly torn and partly pressed from the beans inside by rollers and the jagged punctures of copper sheating on a revolving barrel. In Messrs. Gordon and Co.'s "Single and Double Disc Pulpers" all the parts are strong but light, and may be carried on the backs of mules with ease. They are carefully made and marked, being

"THE COMBINED CRUSHER AND PULPER."

easily put together, and not liable to break down. Worked by hand, the Single Disc Pulper will pulp 30 bushels of ripe Coffee per hour; the Double Disc Pulper will pulp by hand 60 bushels of ripe Coffee per hour. If worked by steam, water, or cattle power, a much larger result would be obtained. The "Double" Pulper of the same firm is more complicated, and being, consequently, liable to breakdowns, can only be recommended where an engineer is at hand in case of a mishap; but their "Combined Coffee Crusher and Pulper" is of excellent design. The cylinder is stoutly cased with copper, and the machine is provided with water hopper and sieve. By addition of the crushing roll, the pulper is rendered more expeditious in operation, and will deliver without damage to the beans from 100 to 120 bushels of cleanly-pulped Coffee per hour. This pulper is adapted for mill work only, and is unsuited for manual labour, being driven by leather belt from shafting connected with water or other power.

But though with good machinery, such as the above, even a new hand can generally save a crop in marketable guise, yet pulping is not always the simple work it may seem. "Successful pulping," we are told, "depends greatly on the dryness of the season or otherwise. One season the Coffee may all be plump and ripe, when pulpers will easily work through 90 to 100 bushels per hour, having plenty of water to run into the machines with the Coffee; the next season may be a dry one, and the trees bearing heavily, very few of the berries become fully ripe. Now the difficulty of pulping commences, the pulp adhering to the parchment owing to the absence of saccharine matter. Should the pulper be 'set close,' it will

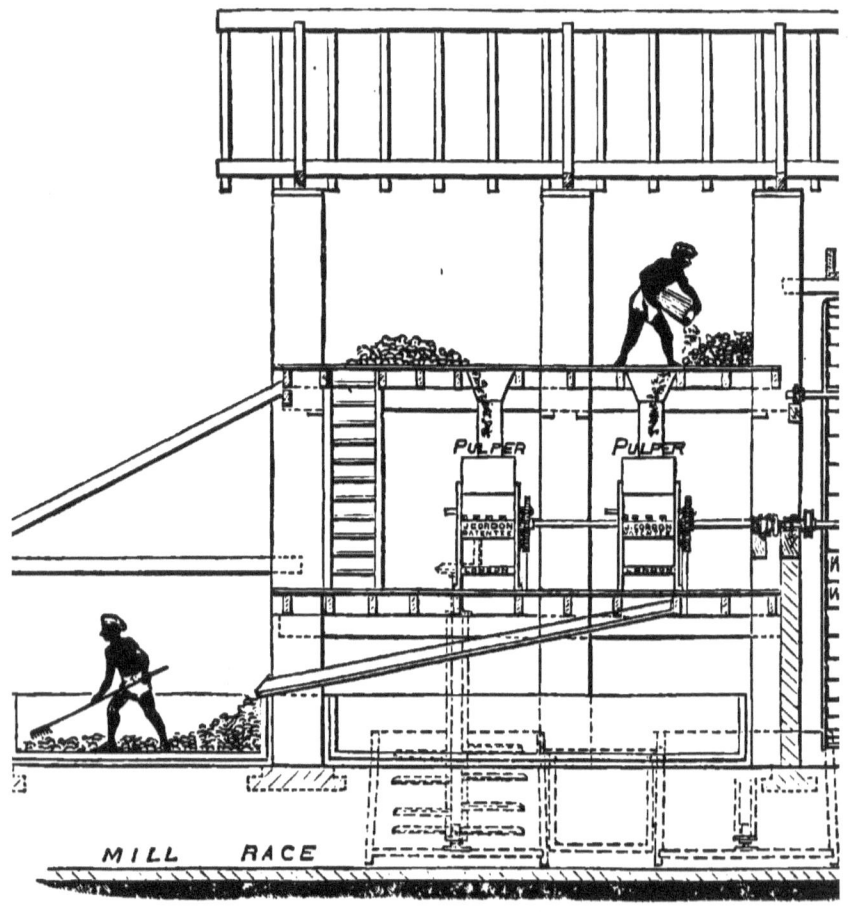

LONGITUDINAL SECTION OF COFFEE MILL.

PULPING AND PREPARING.

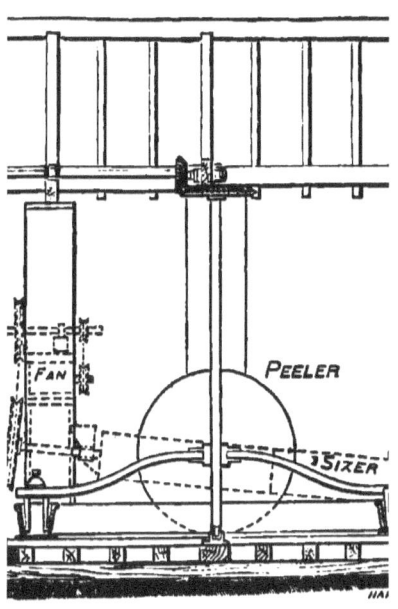

LONGITUDINAL SECTION OF COFFEE MILL.

probably take off the parchment as well as the pulp. The greatest patience will be required, as the same machinery as was used the preceding year will now be unable to pulp more than one-third of the quantity."

From the pulper the Coffee beans are delivered into soaking cisterns, the pulp itself passing away into the mill race, or into a pit for manure. This removes with fermentation any remains of pulp still adhering, and also partly clears the beans of all matter which hangs about the second skin or parchment. Thence it goes into "washers," where a further cleansing process is thoroughly effected by means of stirrers or agitators, which reject not only the mucilage, but any remaining pieces of pulp, and clear away the light unsound Coffee without damage to the beans. The use of the ordinary rake in the cisterns not unfrequently causes breakage of the parchment skin, which is to be avoided before exposing the beans to dry. The Coffee bean, if thus damaged, becomes white, and has to be picked out by hand. When the washing is completed, on raising a small sluice, the seed is discharged on to the draining slope or platform, and is thence passed to the drying ground. It should not dry too quickly, but on a fairly hot day it is spread some two or three inches deep on the hard mat-covered surface of the "barbecues," or drying plots, and constantly turned by bare-footed coolies, who "scuffle" it into rows and trenches. The time occupied in drying will naturally depend much on the weather. The beans should be dried hard and crisp, so that they will crack like a piece of glass between the teeth.

The process of peeling coming next requires great care, its object being the removal of the fine parchment and silver skin which adheres to the bean, without crushing or damaging the bean itself. Perhaps for effectually and quickly peeling Coffee with least amount of breakage, nothing excels a pair of edge-runners, suitably arranged, and with a pan of proper construction. Sixty bushels (equal to 12 cwt. of market Coffee) may be peeled per hour, with scarcely any breakage, with a good machine, while a badly-constructed mill and pan will cause breakage of as much Coffee as it will pass through uninjured. Here a nice adjustment is of the first importance: the dry, delicate and now brittle parchment being cracked from the bean, a final strong winnowing removing the silver skin.

This latter work, however, as well as packing in "jail" bags, or inside charred barrels, is usually done by seaport agents, who have more labour at command than the upland planters; amongst them the period following crop time is always fully occupied in getting the estate into order, pruning, weeding, &c.

Lately the question of whether or not it is

advisable to send Coffee to the European markets in the parchment has been much mooted, and arguing theoretically we should say the weight of reason was all in favour of so sending it.

From a circular of the firm Chabot and Andres at Rotterdam we extract the following:—

According to statistics, the importation of Coffee in the parchment for nine months has been—

For Rotterdam	101,752 bags
For Amsterdam	86,253 bags
	188,095 bags

against about 150,000 bags in the previous year.

It thus appears that the conviction is gaining ground more and more, that sending in the parchment is in the interest of the proprietors. The results obtained this season leave no more doubt about it, and we are persuaded this manner of supply will increase from year to year.

Artificial drying houses are another development of modern scientific planting. They are intended to do away with the dilemma which stares superintendents in the face when they have plucked and pulped their crop, but cannot get a gleam of sunshine (as is often the case in upland regions) for the essential subsequent drying of it.

Most Indian houses, as they are at present, are of no use for drying Coffee and other tropical productions, the temperature in them not being sufficiently equable. To meet all requisites, a drying

house must answer to the following conditions:—
1. Cheapness and simplicity of arrangement, so that it can be fitted up without difficulty by native workpeople. 2. Avoidance of all machinery whatever, which cannot undergo repairs in those mountainous districts, and would require technical supervision. 3. The arrangement must be destined and calculated to dry any required quantity of Coffee. 4. The beans must be all of an equal dryness and hardness, without injuring the colour or the aroma. 5. The use of all kinds of wood and refuse must be practicable for drying purposes, and the least possible quantity of fuel in proportion to the volume to be dried. 6. The escaping air, on leaving the apparatus, must have absorbed the greatest possible quantity of water. 7. The operation should not require any great number of workpeople or close supervision, and must be able to be left to any intelligent coolie.

Mr. Van Maanen is said to have succeeded in compassing all this, and in setting up establishments with which everyone is highly gratified. As to the establishments themselves, they consist in a building which is warmed by flues serving also as smoke conduits. The building is square or oblong, according as the local situation or the quantity of Coffee to be dried may require; and the drying is effected by a supply of outer air, heated by contact with the flues, and which escapes after absorbing the moisture of the Coffee, under and through which the heated air passes as it lies spread out on coarse matting resting upon open rafters.

All this may seem very complicated, or even unintelligible, to those who have not witnessed the work, but a short familiarity with the routine soon renders it intelligible. The gist of the matter is just this: Pick your crop promptly as it ripens, taking the cherries when they are just at their plumpest; allow as little delay as possible to intervene between plucking and pulping (if there must be a delay let the Coffee lie in water tanks); do not overdrive your pulper, whether a time-honoured "rattletrap" or the latest thing out from London; wash clean in the tanks, and dry thoroughly on the barbecues or drying tables.

Coffee stands two days in the fermenting cistern in high districts, but one is sufficient lower down to loosen and soften the sticky remains of pulp.

Under the head of Buildings, the cost of store and pulping house erection is indicated, but no two estate managers follow the same style of architecture. Wattle and daub buildings are half the price of stone and timber ones, while those vary again infinitely according to the supply of crude material. Picking, pulping, and drying say 400 cwt. of Coffee off 100 acres—viz., 4 cwt. at Rs. 3—ought to come under Rs. 1,200. To this must be added rail, water, or cart carriage to the coast, and low country charges, curing, packing, freight, brokerage, &c. It has been calculated our crop loses in the process to clean Coffee 61.75 per cent. of bulk and 81.8 per cent. of weight—that is, 100 lb. of "cherry Coffee" yields not quite 19 lb. of marketable beans. The average product of a ton of parchment Coffee as it comes down by railway, is 12 cwt., so that the reduction at this stage is 40 per cent. Considering the amount of moisture in cherry Coffee, at least 40 per cent. may be lost in pulping. "It is a curious result," someone says, "the weight of the parchment skin should be 1.8 per cent. more than that of the pulp, the loss by pulping being 40 per cent., and again by clearing away the parchment 41.8." Such loss in weight must be remembered when estimating the value of a crop after a first drying. There is also a slight loss in weight again on shipboard.

We have asked the firm before mentioned what would be the approximate cost of a first-class supply of machinery for an estate of 500 to 1,000 acres in full bearing, and annexed is their instructive reply:—

"DASHWOOD HOUSE, 9, NEW BROAD STREET,
"LONDON, 1885.

"DEAR SIR,—In answer to your favour to hand, we beg to say that the price for a plant of machinery to treat the Coffee from 500 to 1,000 acres would be as follows, and consisting of—

- 4 Pulpers, B size,
- 1 Horizontal Washer,
- 1 Double Peeling Mill, 9 ft. and $10\frac{1}{2}$ ft. diameter,
- 1 Fan,
- 1 Combined Separator,
- 3 Elevators, and Shafting, Gearing and Belting to connect to motive power,
- 1 Overshot Water Wheel capable of giving motion to the above machinery, say 18 ft. diameter.

The whole packed and delivered to ship in London, say £610. If a steam engine and boiler were substituted for the water wheel the cost would be some £690.

"Yours truly,

"GORDON & Co."

It need hardly be said good work can be done with a much more moderate outfit.

CHAPTER XVII.

CATTLE AND FODDER.

A HERD of some sort is amongst essential requisites on every estate. Good, strong buffaloes are one of the most valuable forms of "power" at command, and if not quite so cheap and effective as water, are always to hand, which is more than can be said of the other motive power.

For turning pulping machinery, and all the varied work of the curing sheds, for stamping clay for bricks, for drawing water, for dragging light carts over estate roads, or fetching stores and materials from the head of the ghaut, the common Indian beast of burden is unrivalled.

But cattle have another almost more important class of duty, and this is manufacturing manure for the clearings—cattle shed litter, when properly saved and judiciously applied, being as good a manure under the Equator for all kinds of plant life as it is recognised to be in Europe. It is a pity, then, that these invaluable auxiliaries of the planter are not more carefully bred and looked after than is usually the case. In Travancore at least the cattle on the estates seemed to me of poor breeds. The monsoon is too severe for them to thrive, and only West coast cattle or crossbreeds stand the heavy rains; indeed, cattle there did not increase, the births not even keeping up with deaths, and only by frequent purchases could herds be kept up to their full strength. Some estates were trying pigs and various live stock. For manure there is little doubt these animals are almost as good as cattle.

One authority of weight (Mr. Robertson, Commissioner, Central Division) says on this subject:—

"As regards cattle and horses, nothing whatever has been done to improve the breed of cattle, and but little to improve the breed of horses by two or three Government stallions being kept in each Collectorate. The fact is, the people have no good bulls, no good rams, no good horse or donkey stallions. Whenever an animal is ready for the male it finds a mate anywhere in the fields—perhaps the bull or stallion thus used may be a perfectly useless brute; the result is that both horses and cattle are everywhere very poor indeed. It would be well if in each taluka of a Collectorate three or four good bulls were kept, a very small fee being charged for their services. I hold that there never can be any real and permanent improvement in cattle or horses till we go to the root of the evil, and take steps to stop the keeping of useless bulls and stallions."

But Mr. Toynbee takes another view in his Report to the Famine Commissioners (1884), remarking :—

"Ordinary cattle of the country are admirably adapted by nature to its wants, and a sufficient supply of food is all that is required to enable them to do the work required of them and to prevent their deterioration. If larger cattle were successfully bred they would die of starvation, and would be no more useful, even if they lived, than the cattle of the country."

In some districts, of course, there are good herds, and sufficient, but I cannot believe that, taking India as a whole, there is not room for improvement in the gaunt, mongrel, and very "lean kine" who drag the ryots' wooden plough, and meander down the dusty white roads alongside the shaft of his bandy. A little "breeding" would seem to be usually as satisfactory in cattle as in higher ranks of animal life.

For the accommodation of estate herds sheds are requisite. Two great essentials should be observed in the construction of these. Firstly, the securing of the animals' health by cleanliness, warmth, and ventilation; and, secondly, the saving of the litter and droppings, which are removed not less often than once in twenty-four hours.

As a rule bullocks in India are housed without litter, although in some villages it is the practice to litter them in the cold weather with grass or refuse straw, which collects liquid as well as all their solid excrements. The native objection to the practice in the rains is that, even where litter is available, it brings in snakes and insects, and is, on account of the fermentation and heat induced by the climate, injurious to the feet as well as to the general health of cattle. But the greatest objection of all is the absence of available straw or grass, the whole of which is used either as fodder or as fuel. This latter does not apply to many districts.

The plan of letting straw and cow-dung accumulate under foot for days or weeks, and then liberating vast bodies of gases by its removal, though it may secure reasonably good manure, cannot but be hurtful to the unfortunate cattle, and is not to be recommended in a tropical climate.

The opinion of *Mr. Robertson*, of the Sydapet Farm, Madras, whom we have quoted before, differs from ours here; he says:—

"Our manure is made in cattle-boxes under cover, protected alike from sun and rain. It consists of straw used in bedding, and the excrementitious matters of the cattle, which being allowed to accumulate in the boxes during two or three months, layer by layer, and being constantly subjected to the pressure of the animals' feet, becomes a rich homogeneous mass of a dark brown colour, fitted at once for use, without undergoing any preparatory process.

"We find that in an average year we obtain twenty cartloads of this manure for *each* working bullock housed in these boxes; and this is only the manure made at night and during the day when the cattle are not engaged in field labour. Thus, *for every pair of working cattle we employ we can calculate on obtaining forty cartloads per annum* of farmyard manure, or, as it should more strictly be called, box manure.

"We now use this manure *direct* from the cattle-boxes; formerly I had it carefully stacked in pits in the different places in which it would be needed, but I was obliged to give this up, as the manure in a dry season suffered so much, not perhaps by any diminution in its fertilizing ingredients but in its physical properties, for it must be remembered that the beneficial results attending the use of farmyard manure are due to no inconsiderable extent to its physical action on the soil, as well as to its power of yielding to the soil the exact chemical food needed for the production of crops."

A plan very popular in Ceylon, where the art of keeping and utilizing is better understood than elsewhere, is as follows: The byres—much the same as the cattle sheds of an ordinary English homestead, but constructed of wattle and daub, or better still, all chunum—faced stone, placed on somewhat elevated ground, away from dwelling places of natives and Englishmen, but centrally situated in order to facilitate the distribution of manure, are built in parallelograms, each shed being sufficiently broad to contain a double row of animals against the walls, the floors being slightly sloped towards the centre of the building, where a channel of tiles or iron spouting runs its whole length. At the far end is the muck yard, into which the waste material is raked through folding doors every day, the moisture from the sheds coming to the same place, and pigs being kept within the enclosure, whose sharp feet assist the process of decomposition, and reduce the mass to a close, dark-coloured and friable condition. Occasionally this cattle-shed manure, second to none in value and usefulness, is stored in pits filled in succession, those that have stood longest being the first carted away to the clearings or central depot heap. This is a very good arrangement, and it should not be forgotten that in its more liquid part lies the best fertilizing portions of cattle shed litter. These should be saved from draining away, and the muck generally kept as close and compact as possible.

Sometimes native cows are shedded at night with the estate herd, the villagers, if there are any in the neighbourhood, being very ready thus to house their animals upon receiving a small payment, and two purposes are accomplished thereby. In the first place, a great addition is made to the nightly outturn of manure; and in the second, the overseer has the satisfaction of knowing that the coolies' kine are under lock and key, not straying amongst his Coffee or nurseries—a thing that is only too likely to happen otherwise. These stallers will want feeding. In the daytime, those that are not employed upon useful work go to open hillsides under charge of a cow-boy, or even cow-woman, there enjoying themselves amongst the lemon grass and short brushwood. But artificially-cultivated fodder has to be provided in every case for stall feeding, and according to the number of head kept.

Guinea grass is one of the best green food plants. When the grass is established, it needs no more attention, but in a good situation affords a continual cut of hay for cattle, without any trouble expended in return. In forming a field, the only thing necessary is to secure a wet week or ten days for the operation, which is briefly as follows: —The roots of the grass from some old-established estate having been brought into the clearing, previously freed from weeds, stones, and branches, so far as may be, are torn into bunches, each of which should have about twelve stems. Coolies, armed with mamôties, then dig or scrape little holes in the ground, as much as possible in lines, and about eighteen inches apart. In these the second line of coolies, usually women or boys, place the roots, but instead of planting them upright, divide each bunch, and, when inserting them in the holes, bend half the stems one way and half the other—an arrangement which is supposed to make the plant spread more and cover the ground. In this way, when the field is completely covered, all care is over, for if the rain continues for a few days after the planting, the roots will strike, and the young shoots, coming up strong and thick, will cloak the rugged "clearing" with a deep green carpet, which in a wet season will in three or four months be tall enough to hide a man. It is not, however, allowed to reach that height, but is cut with a sickle when about eighteen inches high.

In a recent report Mr. Robertson said the area of land under this valuable fodder plant has been considerably extended, and the better he became acquainted with the grass the more he valued it. He had very fine crops which had never been irrigated, and some of the best results he obtained in fattening stock were obtained with guinea grass. The fodder can be used for all kinds of beasts; it seems to disturb the digestive organs of some animals, but this is only temporary. I have fed cattle and sheep on it *exclusively* for *months*, not only without ill effects, but with the most satisfactory results. I have found our guinea-grass field a capital place in which to graze our working cattle during the hot season, and for the ewes with young lambs I could scarcely desire a better pasture. It produces such an abundant flow of milk in the ewes without (what is common in such cases) disturbing the health of either mother or lamb.

"Prickly Comfrey" is another wonderfully prolific green crop. The Russian variety, on favourable soil, will give as much as 150 tons per acre, and it is much liked by cattle. It requires, however, a good, deep earth, and a rather damp location.

With regard to yellow cholum (*sorghum vulgare*), this valuable fodder crop is yet but little appreciated by those who might benefit most largely by cultivating it. Most of the live stock on the Sydapet farms are fed on cholum fodder throughout a greater part of the year. It is chiefly a lowland cultivation, but as it produces, under favourable circumstances, as much as nineteen tons per acre, it is worth a trial wherever there is spare land of moderate depth and goodness.

Chinese sugar-cane, which was introduced from Sydney in the early part of 1870, had established itself as one of the regular cold-weather crops.

"Cumbo" is a plant chiefly serviceable for supplying good fodder during the hot months of May, June, and July. Horse grain and "paddy" are also grown for the estate live stock.

It must not be forgotten that, according to a principle well understood among British farmers, since the value of bullock-dung as a manure depends on the quality of the food given to the cattle, and the latter is in India usually of poor character, consisting as it does merely of chopped straw, it follows that the value of the muck-heap manure is very much less than that of the same weight of farmyard muck in Europe. The chief exception to the rule is in cotton-growing tracts where much cotton seed is utilised as cattle food, and cotton seed is one of the most valuable manure producers which exists.

All estate herds, then, should be well fed not only with nutritious green crops, but with good oil cake, grain, &c. Fat cattle on an estate speak well for its future crops.

CHAPTER XVIII.

MANURES AND MANURING.

For new estates neither manure nor manurings ought to be necessary for some time, since the soil should be so deep and rich in virgin fertility that the plants will grow and thrive without artificial stimulation. It is when estates are being drawn upon heavily, or past their prime, say from ten to twenty years old, according to soil, their resources begin to fail, and have to be made good by imported materials. Besides this exhaustion from simple usage, there is the other one wherein a condition of practical barrenness is produced by removal of fine top soil, following upon "wash" caused by the exterminating of trees and undergrowth over hill ranges, as previously mentioned.

To prevent "wash" (the most rudimentary process in preserving a garden in a state of productiveness), we have one system of drainage with frequent channels, run—slightly downwards—across the face of the slopes and into the nearest watercourse. These preserve our top soil, and save any manure we may put on from being swept away. There is another kind of drain sometimes useful in drawing water from hollow and swamps. If land would need draining for any ordinary cereal crop, it must undoubtedly be drained for Coffee. "Wet feet" is an ailment the latter plant is especially sensitive to. All "sour" land must be thoroughly reclaimed, and if that is not possible except at great expense, then the next best thing is to abandon it.

This, however, is not a matter that need cause much uneasiness, as very little Coffee soil in India or Ceylon suffers from stagnant water. Such spots of course there are upon every garden, but they are usually abandoned to nature, who rears crops of her own sowing upon them.

Serving the same purpose of conserving soil is the system by which *water holes*, previously mentioned, are dotted over the clearings. "These," we are told, "were first introduced as holes intended to be filled with manure. The article, however, running short the holes remained open, and it was found after some time that the tree took a fresh start of growth, partly, perhaps, caused by the temporary exposure of the roots to the sun and air, and partly by the loose earth that gradually dribbled into the hole again, together with whatever accumulations of leaves, timber and other decayed vegetable matter lay about on the surface of the ground near. It has since become a system to make water holes between every four trees, or between every eight or twelve trees. These are generally made about 2 feet square by 1 foot deep, or 20 inches square by 18, according to taste and space. If the object be to collect water and save wash, the more holes the better; while if it be in a dry district, and intended to catch the accumulated surface *débris*, fewer will do, and the earth taken from them may with advantage be thrown back on to the exposed stems of the bushes, where it will do good service."

Having thus noted how the water must be got rid of and soil protected where the land is steep and exposed to wear and tear of wind and rain by trenches, water holes, or such like contrivances, we may turn to the question of manuring proper. This subject has a full and learned literature of its own. Nothing but the popular and generally-received results of much experiment and expenditure can be brought within the limits of a few pages. The action of various manures upon the complicated structure of our plants, and their fine chemical properties, cannot be gone into in so practical a manual as this. A mere enumeration of those which have been found the most serviceable is all our limits will allow. Such a list includes—

Cattle manure.

Other animal manures.

Poonac and bones (in proportion of two to one in weight).

Bones and guano.

Coffee pulp.
Pulp and lime.
Cattle manure and pulp.
Bones and pulp.
Bones, pulp, and guano.
Sombreorum (a concentrated artificial manure).
Fish.
Ashes.
Animal charcoal.
Phosphoric potash.
Sal-ammoniac and poonac.
Sulphate of ammonia.
Dissolved bones and swamp soil.
Compost of cattle manure, bones, pulp, Coffee husk, and mana grass.
Compost of vegetable matter saturated with diluted sulphate of ammonia.
Compost of poonac (1 cwt.), bone dust (½ cwt.), Bolivian guano (¼ cwt.)
Compost of pulp, lime, and mud and manure from drains.
Compost of poonac (five-eighths), bones (two-eighths), guano (one-eighth).

These are some, but by no means all, of the manures that have been tried and have found patrons amongst managers, the planters of Ceylon being especially energetic in their researches for new fertilizing compounds and composts, a result no doubt due to the demand which their somewhat overworked soil has made, since 1867, upon their ingenuity.

A report by a Committee of the Ceylon Planters' Association (though the report is by this time far down on the Association's file of memorandum) gives some sensible advice on general application of all such manures, and so tersely it is difficult to put it in better language than the originals.

"The best mode of application," we read, "seems to be to place the bulky manures in holes from, say, 1½ feet square, and in depth from 6 inches to 18 inches, and 6 to 18 inches from the stem of the tree; the artificial manures being placed in smaller holes of less depth. On some estates the plan seems to have succeeded of placing a large quantity of pulp (five baskets) in holes cut in a space between every four trees, at a cost of £9 per acre." The quantities of the several manures used are as follows :—

"Phosphoric potash, ½ lb. to tree; bonedust and poonac, ¾ lb. to 1½ lb. per tree; cattle dung, 1 basketful to 3 baskets (30 lb.); sombreorum, 4 to 7 oz.; bones, ¾ lb. to 1 lb.

Composts :—	Pulp, lime, and ravine soil, 1. ½ lb. lime, 1 bushel pulp.
Do.	1 bushel ravine soil.
Do.	Dissolved bones 1 lb., and swamp soil 1 basket.
Do.	Bolivian guano, ½ lb.; Peruvian, ¼ lb.; and bones, ¼ lb.
Do.	Cattle manure, 1 basket; guano, 3 oz."

Of other manures the cost, as can be gathered from the reports, is as follows:—

"Artificial manures, £6 2s. per acre; bones and poonac, £5 10s. to £8 per acre; sombreorum, £3 to £6 10s. per acre; bonedust and ashes, £10 to £12 per acre; poonac, bonedust, and Bolivian guano, £7 2s. per acre; poonac, bonedust, and good guano, £6 15s. 3d. per acre; pulp, £1 16s. 6d. to £2 10s. per acre."

Of the relative effects of the manures, the following seems to be the result deducible from the majority of these enquiries:—

"That cattle manure is *par excellence* the best and most lasting, the effects remaining over two to three years. Next in order come bones and poonac, which are held to be good from one to two years. Guano alone is considered too stimulating and not lasting, but in mixtures (in small quantities) with bones and poonac seems to have a very beneficial effect. Several of the writers speak very favourably of the application of pulp."

The Sub-Committee make the following suggestions with regard to mode and time of application of manure:—

"First, that all lands except such as have little or no slope should, in the first instance, be carefully drained; that bulky manures should be placed in holes of not less size than 2 feet by 1 foot, and not exceeding 1 foot in depth, and at a distance of from 9 to 18 inches from the stem of the tree. That artificial manures should be in semicircular holes above the tree, and of smaller size."

The Committee's advice is excellent, but it may be noted the price of artificial manures has cheapened somewhat of late, as the means of getting them up country have been greatly improved by new lines of railway, new roads, bridges, &c.

Planters also at the present time make (with good reason) their pits for bulky manures between the Coffee trees larger than formerly, and artificial manures are not put into small holes in their natural strength to scorch all rootlets they come in contact with, but are mixed largely with jungle soil and spread round the stems in shallow "pans" —*i.e.*, light depressions in the ground—afterwards covered over with a little earth.

In applying farmyard manure, care should be taken to see it is covered up completely in the holes about the trees. The liquid portion is rather more valuable than the bulky, as the following analysis shows.

The approximate composition of urine and dung of well-fed cattle is as follows:—

	Urine.	Dung.
Water	920	840
(a) Organic matter, urea, uric acid, &c.	60	135
(b) Inorganic matter, salts of potash, soda, &c.	20	25
Total	1,000	1,000
(a) Containing nitrogen capable of yielding ammonia	9.00	3.60
(b) Containing phosphoric acid	.70	2.25

It will be seen, as noted before, which is the most valuable fertilizing agent, and that cattle yard "muck" suffers a serious loss from urine being allowed to run to waste. Much loss there is also caused in India by the solid excrements being used as a fuel for the whole of the organic matter, which constitutes at least 85 per cent. of dry dung, and which contains, amongst other valuable plant food, a large per-centage of nitrogen, the most costly and most difficult to replace of all these foods, is then dissipated into air and lost. Nor is any economy secured by using cow-dung for fuel, since the selling price of a ton of dry dung is, in most instances, in excess of the selling price of firewood, and, at the least, double the price at which firewood could be produced in the neighbourhood of towns, and on the holdings of ryots for their household use.

"In Hindoostan the dung-heap is never under cover, and is exposed to heat, wind, and rain. The consequence is that all gaseous ammonia is expelled by the solar heat, and dispersed by the wind; the rain washes out all soluble fertilizing matters from the dung-heap, and that which remains is the solid and least valuable part of the manure, being composed of the undigested fibres of the hay and grass consumed by the animal as food. This shows how necessary it is to make and preserve manure under cover."—*J. F. Pogson.*

As litter for cattle, perhaps, the common bracken would be better in some cases than hill grasses, or general vegetable refuse.

This fern (Pteris Aguilina), generally known as the bracken, is found abundantly in many parts of the higher hill ranges of the Madras Presidency. It is used as a litter for cattle stalls very largely by Coffee planters resident on the Neilgherries, in Wynaad and in Coorg. For this purpose it is well suited when the straw of cereals is costly and difficult to obtain. Used in cattle boxes, the fern

	Bracken.	Wheat Straw.
Per cent. of ash ...	7.01	4.95
COMPOSITION OF THE ASH.		
Potash	42.8	11.5
Soda	4.5	2.9
Magnesia	7.7	2.6
Lime	14.0	6.2
Phosphoric acid ...	9.7	5.4
Sulphuric acid ...	5.1	2.9
Silica	6.0	68.3
Chlorine	10.2	—
Total	100.	99.8

rots more readily than in ordinary byres; it is used chiefly in the large open "crawls" in which buffaloes and hill cattle are confined at night. These "crawls" are kept liberally bedded with ferns, grass, &c., which, under the treading of the cattle at night, aided by rain, become broken up and worked into a black-coloured mass. This is a convenient and expeditious way of converting ferns into a form convenient for manuring.

The preceding table gives an analysis of the composition of the ash of the bracken, compared with an average analysis of wheat straw.

It will be observed, in comparing these analyses, that not only does the fern yield a much larger quantity of ash than wheat straw, but that more than one-half of this ash consists of the highly-valuable fertilizing substances phosphoric acid and potash—both so essential in a soil on which Coffee trees are growing.

Cattle manure we look upon as one of the best manures known, even in this day of scientific research. There is no question but that it is bulky, and consequently expensive to use; on some estates, indeed, it is never collected for this reason. But by placing your cattle-sheds with forethought on your roads, centrally, and moderately high up, so that the manure is, if possible, taken *down* to the Coffee, the fertilizer should be made and spread, we think, at about Rs. 50 per acre, according to facilities of grazing, transport of bedding, carriage, &c., &c. Manuring with cattle-dung, aided by bone-dust or artificial manure, Mr. Sabonadière believes, could be so managed that, with an average expenditure of £3 (Rs. 30) per acre per annum, " properties of even medium soil might be kept to an average bearing rate of 8 to 10 cwts. an acre, which would fully repay the cost, and leave a large profit besides." Sweepings from stables, roads, bazaars, sheepfolds, chicken-runs, should all find their way to the heap where "line" sweepings and night soil are collected. This *poudrette* consists of village ashes and the excrementitious matters collected daily from the village latrines. Care was taken to have ashes thrown over the mounds. After remaining in heaps thus formed for six or eight months, the manure became thoroughly deodorized and fit for use. In this state coolies make no objection whatever to work with it; and the character of the manure is so thoroughly changed that few persons could, from its appearance, determine the nature of its original ingredient. It will be more available under some circumstances than others, but should never be neglected.

Though not a usual source of manure, bat guano is sometimes to be had, and nothing could be better in its way. The great Indian fruit bats, who sally forth at sunset in regiments and battalions, spend the hours of daylight in clefts in rocks and hanging to the roofs of caverns. The droppings, accumulated for centuries, below them are sometimes two or three feet thick, and then well worth removing and using as an artificial stimulant.

Among other substances there is castor oil cake, especially rich in nitrogen; it is, therefore, a powerful fertilizer. Its action is slow, but when mixed with cattle manure it becomes a great deal more active and more fitted to meet the wants of quick growing crops. For Coffee and Tea plantations a more useful auxiliary manure can scarcely be obtained. This costs about Rs. 15½ per ton, delivered in Madras or Colombo, and perhaps 200 lbs. per acre would be an average allowance.

Cotton seed, which had been steeped in urine or water to destroy its vitality, is again undoubtedly one of the best manures we possess, and is suited for any crop that will grow. In cotton seed we have a large quantity of fertilizing matter concentrated in a very little bulk. It is thus well suited for planters, and where, in order to reduce the cost of transit, it is necessary to get a *portable concentrated manure.*

All the different preparations of bones are valuable, whether as boiled bones, crushed bones, bone dust, bone black, or in the form of superphosphate, chiefly in yielding phosphate of lime. Though in the *raw state* bones yield a large percentage of ammonia, still it is as a means of adding phosphate of lime to the soil they are chiefly employed, as it is phosphoric acid and phosphate of lime that all cultivated crops appropriate so largely. Bones are costly in India, but there seems little probability of their becoming cheaper, as their use is becoming much more general, especially amongst Tea and Coffee planters on the hills. "Our only hope of obtaining phosphatic materials at a fair price," observe the

Famine Commissioners, "is in the discovery of phosphatic rocks, or coprolites, in accessible parts of each agricultural district."

Sawdust is said to have a wonderful effect on garden crops, and experiments might be made on a few bushes with some from the nearest sawpit. Wood ashes are rich in potash and phosphoric acid. The prunings of the bushes with the lighter weeds buried in trenches between the rows tend also to keep up the fertility of the soil, as do the leaves falling from shade trees, and the annual clearings out of drains, water holes, &c.

Lime, though not strictly speaking a manure, is of the utmost value in many soils. We obtain this in the form of burnt shells, marine and fresh water, such as are used for preparing shell chunam. They yield an almost pure carbonate of lime, containing an exceedingly small quantity of impurities. After being slacked it forms a light powder, which can with great facility be used on the land; or if an estate is deficient in this generally abundant element, it is replaced in the form of gypsum, or native lime stone.

Professor E. W. Hilgard, in discussing the "Objects and Interpretation of Soil Analyses," rives, among other things, the following advantages resulting from an adequate supply of this mineral in soils:—1. A more rapid transformation of vegetable matter into active humus, which manifests itself by a dark or deep black tint of the soil.

2. The retention of such humus, against the oxidizing influences of hot climates. 3. Whether through the medium of this humus, or in a more direct manner, it renders adequate for profitable culture per-centages of phosphoric acid and potash so small that in the case of deficiency or absence of lime the soil is practically sterile. 4. It tends to secure the proper maintenance of the conditions of nitrification, whereby the inert nitrogen of the soil is rendered available. 5. It exerts a most important physical action on the flocculation, and therefore on the "freeness" and permeability of soils. Or if put more simply, a free application of lime, at the rate of perhaps 1 lb. to a tree, enables plants to draw upon all the resources of a soil which otherwise might be locked up from them.

Of Coffee pulp as a manure we do not ourselves think much, though we know it has been highly spoken of. No doubt it should not be altogether wasted, but may well go to form the basis of some useful compost.

There is yet another manure indigenous to estates which must not be overlooked. This is *mana* grass, a tall species of its family growing luxuriantly upon most hillsides just beyond the forest line. It is cut, brought down, and the ground between the rows thickly thatched at the rate of perhaps a coolie-load to a bush—undoubtedly a costly work, but one paying well on heavy, cold, clay lands. It keeps down weeds, is practically a cure for the black bug blight, and has a very favourable effect upon some earths, though, according to Liebig, in analysis this grass shows only in its ash 3 per cent. of potash and 2 of chloride of potassa against $81\frac{1}{2}$ of silica. The effect of the grass is important enough to justify us in letting one of its most enthusiastic users speak in its behalf:—

"Mana grass is most useful, both as bedding for cattle and a litter to be applied on the surface of the soil. When used for the former purpose its chief advantages are its abundance, and the facility with which it may be cut and carried. When applied to free soils that abound in vegetable matter it is scarcely of any use except to keep down weeds or to kill running grass; but on cold, wet soils its effect is almost magical, exceeding that of a heavy dose of cattle manure. I have applied it to a cold, heavy, yellow soil, in which Coffee bushes could scarcely exist, and where their scraggy branches had only a few small yellow leaves on them, and the effect was most surprising. Not only were the trees soon clothed with fine dark green foliage, but even the soil appeared to be changed, and, to the depth of three or four inches, became friable and dry. How this change was accomplished, whether by the acids resulting from the decomposition of the grass, or by the protection afforded to the soil, I do not pretend to say, but I can speak confidently to the fact.

"*Effect.*—The increase of crop obtained through the agency of this manure, in the instance above alluded to, was at least 5 cwt. per acre.

"*Cost.*—The cost of this method of manuring is much less felt on a weedy estate than on a clean one, because on the former it almost supersedes the necessity for weeding. The principal item of cost is the carriage of the grass. I have, therefore, restricted the use of mana grass to places within one hundred trees of the spot where the grass is grown. Under this system the cost of a heavy littering, in which each tree has a very heavy coolie-load of grass, is 35s. per acre. One such heavy littering, and two light ones of about 20s. per acre each, are sufficient for a year, that is, about 75s. per acre per annum for weeding and manuring. I am of opinion that, after two or three years of this treatment, the land would be able to bear several successive crops without requiring the assistance of litter."

A danger of this litter-manuring is that of fire. Burying the stuff in trenching might be a remedy, or leaving every 20th to 24th row unlittered would confine a chance fire to a limited area.

When we come to the subject of artificial manures, intended to replace those substances of which the land shall stand in need, we come indeed to an extensive subject—one upon which discussion has raged for twenty years and is still raging. The chief elements required by all crops are phosphoric acid, potash, magnesia, and nitrogen: the latter either in the form of nitric acid, as it exists in nitrates of soda and potash, or ammonia, as in sulphates and muriates of ammonia, or in the form of organic nitrogen, as in bones, blood, and other animal refuse.

"What," we recently asked of an Ipswich firm which supplies concentrated fertilizers to estates in all parts of the world, "is the form of fertilizer most generally appreciated and demanded by your clients?" Replying, they say:—

"DEAR SIR,—In answer to your enquiries, we invariably advise our friends to purchase superphosphate, and have added to it, at the estate in India or elsewhere, Bengal saltpetre, which should be obtained there on the most advantageous terms. *There is no better manure for Coffee than one-third Bengal saltpetre and two-thirds patent superphosphate.* As, however, sulphate of ammonia is at the present moment remarkably cheap, it might answer to have a mixture made *of superphosphate, sulphate of potash, and sulphate of ammonia in equal proportions.* This would make a very concentrated manure, and would give satisfactory results. The prices of these ingredients are as follows:—

	PER TON.
Patent superphosphate, containing 45 per cent. of phosporic acid at 6s. 6d. per unit... ...	£14 12 6
Sulphate of potash, 90 per cent. ... =	£10 10 0
Sulphate of ammonia, containing 24 per cent. ammonia ... ... =	£11 15 0

"All manures for Coffee contain, or should contain, the above suggested ingredients; and the proportion we recommend is based upon the constituents of the plant, and which would probably give the best result upon the land."

Artificially-prepared manures, it may be generally said, are more stimulating in their action than likely to do permanent good. They require for their economical application considerable study of the character of the soil and knowledge of the history of previous manurings that may have been carried out. "For pulling a crop through, or putting wood on trees deficient in leaf, such manures as sulphate of ammonia in small quantities may sometimes be used with success," remarks Mr. W. D. Bosanquet; and Mr. Henry Tolputt, the observant manager and courteous director, holds that "ammonia, phosphoric acid, and potash in some form or other, and in due proportions, are what we have to combine to form a perfect manure."

All patent commercial specialities with high-sounding names are but more or less practical realizations of this. Their great advantage is their compactness, allowing the planter to order exactly what his land wants. When the "artificial" is on the estate it can be mixed with jungle soil and applied according to needs.

Of the manner of this application we have already said something. It may either be in holes directly under the trees, or in holes equal distance between every four. Ourselves we prefer the former plan, though by the latter the roots are less likely to be disturbed or injured.

Then there is the question of the best period for putting down manure. Usually it is done before crop time to bring on the fruit, but manure for the blossoming season as well as for crop is really as much required. Flowering is an exhaustive process, requiring a large amount of nourishment, and the sugar planter is so well aware of this that he cuts his canes before they blossom, lest the process should exhaust the juice and therefore rob him of his labour and profits. Towards the end of the rains is probably as good a time as any for forking or holing in heavy stuff.

To sum up. The planters of Ceylon have been thus catechised on the subject, and it should be pointed out, every answer is the result of separate and individual experience and observation.

Question 1st.—What manure gives the best and what the worst results?

Answers:—

1. Cattle manure or sombreorum the best, cocoanut poonac the worst.
2. Best, plain bones or bones and sulphate of ammonia; worst, cocoanut poonac.
3. Cattle manure and bone dust or steamed bones the best; blood and guano the worst.
4. Bone dust and steamed bones the best; castor-poonac the worst.
5. Bones and cattle manure the best.
6. Cattle manure, bones and poonac and Cross' manure.
7. Cattle manure, bones and wood ashes the best; Peruvian guano the worst.
8. Cattle manure and bones as bulk the best.
9. Cattle manure and bones the best; bone meal and cocoanut poonac next best.
10. Cattle manure best; lime worst.
11. Cattle manure the best; vegetable stuff and lime the worst.

Question 2nd.—What mode of application have you found to answer best?

Answers:—

1. For artificial, semi-circular holes above tree; bulk, square holes between every four trees.
2. Saucer-shaped holes dug with a fork and scraped out with hand.
3. Soluble manure scratched in on surface; and regular manuring semicircular hole one foot from tree.
4. Circular holes for artificial, and square for bulk.
5. Generally holing, but occasionally digging.
6. Circular holes.

7. Forking.
8. Close to the tree, must be varied in its application.
9. Holing the best. Digging gives the quickest results.
10. Cutting large holes between four trees.

Question 3rd.—What months have you found to be the best for the application of (*a*) bulky manure, (*b*) artificial? In answering the above questions, kindly give the approximate cost of cultivation, including manure, also the elevation and exposure of the fields in question, as well as the age of the Coffee, with any other information, such as the weather report of the blossom seasons, that you think may be useful.

Answers :—

1. Cost of manure and application, Rs. 45 per acre.
2. August and September the best for artificial; cost, Rs. 45 to Rs. 50 per acre. Cattle manure applied August and September, and cost Rs. 90 to Rs. 100.
3. Bulky manure, January; artificial, April, May. Cost of bulky, Rs. 50 to Rs. 60; artificial, Rs. 40 to Rs. 50.
4. Regular manuring immediately after crop.
5. Cattle manure, January; artificial manure, April and May. Cost: cattle manure, Rs. 80 per acre; artificial, Rs. 45. The oldest Coffee is the best, and fields with eastern exposure give nearly all the crops.
6. Bulk, January and February, and prunings buried. Artificial, June and July. Cost of cultivation, including manure but not superintendence, crop expenses, Rs. 47 per acre; artificial manure, cost Rs. 50; bulk, Rs. 55.
7. Cattle manure, June to August; cost of application, Rs. 25.
8. Early in season before end of April; cost of manure, Rs. 60 to Rs. 70; applied, Rs. 12 to Rs. 15.
9. Bulky manure as soon as possible after blossoming season; artificial, April to August. Cattle manure, cost applied, Rs. 70; artificial, Rs. 48 to 50. Total expenditure, Rs. 120 per acre.

10. Early manuring, January to June ; cost of cultivation with cattle manure, Rs. 150; artificial, Rs. 125 ; and average cost of estate, Rs. 110.

11. Bulky manure, January ; artificial, April and May ; cost cultivation of fields, Rs. 90 to Rs. 100.

Cattle manure, costing Rs. 120 per acre, has given 4 cwt. increase for 3 years; bone dust, costing less, has given $4\frac{1}{2}$ cwt. per acre first year, and 2 cwt. the second year; bones and poonac, at Rs. 85 per acre, have improved crop to the extent of 4 cwt. for two years; sombreorum, at Rs. 50, should effect an improvement of 3 to 4 cwt.; and animal refuse, line sweepings, &c., at Rs. 80 per acre, should represent an increase of 2 to 4 cwt. But the nature of the original soil will always influence such results. Personally I believe in carefully saved cattle-shed stuff twice in three years, with perhaps a little concentrated artificial manure for emergencies. A yearly expenditure of Rs. 30 to Rs. 40 should cover this.

CHAPTER XIX.

COST AND PROFIT.

WERE we to say at once that it is rash to think of embarking in the Coffee-planting enterprise *without at least £5,000 at command*, there is no doubt but that we should dispel a good many pleasant fancies, and cause, perhaps, a considerable fall in the hopes of the inexperienced. Yet we doubt if a smaller figure than that mentioned above can be taken as safely covering cost of land, initial expenses, and the multitude of contingencies arising during the long period of waiting before any crop is realised.

Under separate chapters we have suggested these various costs arising from different works; it may be as well to bring these together, in yearly headings, and thus see how much we shall be out of pocket before we receive from our lowland brokers that delightful and ever-memorable "first cheque" for a maiden crop.

To begin with, however, we must say that the price of land varies so much and so recklessly, according to fancy or fashion, not only in Ceylon, but in other countries where speculation should be less rife, that it is best not to include it in the estimates. From £2 to £3 (Rs. 20 to 30, however) may be taken as a reasonable equivalent of good forest land. This price will rise to Rs. 50, 100, or even 200, if the plot is very conveniently situated for water, carriage, &c., or if there are rich and prosperous gardens near by. From native states, again, sometimes it can be had at a sum which is merely the recognition of the transfer of rights; and the public auctions held under British rule will vary greatly in their result according to competition.

Approximate Estimates for bringing into bearing 200 acres of Forest Land.

First Year.

(100 ACRES OPENED.)

	Total Rs.
The land having been acquired, there will be, to begin with, surveyor's fees, cutting out, and clearing the first hundred acres, @ Rs. 3 per acre	300
Felling and clearing 100 acres by contract or otherwise, @ Rs. 25 per acre	2,500
Cutting pegs for lining will depend on number of pegs required according to distance the bushes are to be apart. Say we need 187,500, this should be about 14 an. per acre	80
Lining, very variable work may be taken at Rs. 3. The better the burn, the closer the land is cleared, the lighter this and all subsequent works become	300
Carried forward ... ... Rs.	3,180

COST AND PROFIT. 217

	Total Rs.
Brought forward	3,180

Holing should be done well, and not hurried or scamped, as we have pointed out. In round numbers, with 1,500 holes to the acre, the cost will be at least Rs. 16 per acre   1,600

"Filling in," &c., at Rs. 16 per acre   600

Planting and supplying are works second to none in importance of those dealing directly with the bushes. Both require constant supervision and the best labour on the estate. Planting may be taken at Rs. 24 per acre, and supply, if the previous work was done well, Rs. 3; together Rs. 27 per acre   2,700

Tools must not be overlooked. They should all be the best of their kind and English make. Mamoties, alavangas, axes, bill-hooks, pruning knives, water cans, buckets, spades, &c., &c., are amongst the chief required. A careful record should be kept of all issued from the stores every day, or they will be hidden and lost with inconceivable rapidity. There is constant work for one coolie (Sundries) rehandling axes, mamoties, and perhaps for another sharpening and grinding   300

A nursery plot of about an acre may cost to level, clear, plant, and drain Rs. 150. To this should be added the cost of 4 bushels of seed Coffee, Rs. 10 per bushel... ...   190

Lines must be built, and though any sort of miserable shedding is considered good enough for the first year or two, we can

| Carried forward ... ... | Rs. 8,570 |

	Total Rs.
Brought forward	8,570

see no valid reason why these buildings should not be decent and efficient from the first. Ten-roomed lines—stone pillar and shingle—each room 12 by 10, and well made, as previously pointed out, can be put up for about Rs. 550 to 700, say...   600

A bungalow for the Englishman is often not built until the third year, the estate in the meantime being managed through a neighbouring planter, who rides over to superintend. But suppose the owner lives on the land from the first, then a very convenient, if unpretentious, house on stone foundations with shingle roof can be built for Rs. 1,000. Ourselves we should be inclined to add another thousand rupees, and make it very complete, but we accept the lower estimate   1,000

Roads deserve the earliest consideration we can give them. When made *at once*, although it may be not to their full width, they will save 5 per cent. on all subsequent operations. They are necessary but expensive luxuries, costing little under Rs. 140 per mile, and 1½ miles per hundred acres opened is not too much   210

Draining has to be seen to, and the sooner the better. Forty acres of the steepest land—*i.e.*, that in most danger of loosing its soil—at Rs. 7 per acre, will be   280

Carried forward ... ... Rs. 10,660

	Total Rs.
Brought forward	10,660
Weeding as we have seen is light for the first year. Ten runs over the clearings in that period will be sufficient, and these at R. 1 per acre monthly will be	100
Finally there will be the *salary of superintendent*, Rs. 1,000 (at least), to set against the estate	1,000
And *contingencies*. These are apt to increase unduly. They may be said to include a host of items, such as Government medical assessment, taxes, " writer," if there is one, general transport, loss on rice, subscriptions, absenting coolies, &c., &c.	500
Probable expenditure to end of first year Rs.	12,260

Second Year.

	Total Rs.
If we now bring under cultivation the other hundred acres, felling and clearing, pegs, lining, holing, filling in, planting and supplying, &c., as previously, if done in the *best* style, will be not much under	7,780
More lines for coolies will be required, say 60 × 20	700
Another 1½ miles of roads	210
Planting grass for cattle	300
Drains again as last year	280
Tools to replace those lost and broken	100
Weeding: 1st clearing for 12 months, 2nd clearing for 6 months, at Rs. 1 per month	1,800
Superintendence	1,000
Contingencies	500
Probable expenditure to end of second year Rs.	12,670

Third Year. Total Rs.

Much of the work is the same as previously.

Weeding 200 acres 2,400

Upkeep of roads and drains, at Rs. 2 400

Pruning has now to be attended to. Suckering was probably commenced with the monthly weeding about the middle of the last twelve months, but was not heavy enough to need special mention. *Topping* took place at the same time, and cost Rs. 1 = Rs. 200. *Pruning and handling*, at Rs. 4 per acre (including the burying of the rubbish between the rows), with this will be 1,000

This year a *resident manager* will be needed on the estate. £200 (Rs. 2,000) is the usual commencing salary 2,000

Pulping machinery, pulping house and stores, may, as has been shown, cost anything, from Rs. 1,800 for very temporary arrangements, to Rs. 10,000, or even more. Rs. 5,000 ought to set small estates up well, avoiding on the one hand useless display in buildings, and on the other "cutcha" arrangements, sure to end in loss and disappointment 5,000

Picking, pulping, and *drying,* say 400 cwt. off 100 acres, viz., 4 cwt. at Rs. 3, will come to 1,200

Carried forward ... ... Rs. 12,000

	Total Rs.
Brought forward	12,000
Transport to lowlands very likely 8 annas per bushel on 1,900 bushels of "parchment" would equal	950
Contingencies	500
General transport of stores, material, &c. ...	500
Third year ... ... Rs.	13,950

	Rs.
Expenditure—First year	12,260
,, Second year	12,670
,, Third year	13,950
Total expenditure to first crop	38,880
Less value of 400 cwt. at 70s. per cwt. ...	14,000
Estate Dr. ... ... Rs.	24,880

There are several items that have not been taken into consideration here, but they are all such as can be reserved for consideration of a third and fourth year. Nothing has been said about cattle sheds or manure pits. Sheds may be taken as costing about the same price as substantial coolie lines of the same dimensions if built as they ought to be. Coffee spouting, again, has not been mentioned, as it is an "improvement" rarely to be found on a garden during the first few years of its existence. Loss by exchange (due to the fact that the English standard is gold, while that of India is fluctuating silver) is a serious matter, a loss in fact of some six per cent. or more; and though the rupee is nominally worth 2s. sterling, it has for a long time only represented 1s. 7d. to 1s. 10d., 1s. 8d. being about the actual value it can be relied upon as indicating. Nor has anything been allowed for the interest of the money invested, while of course there are the personal expenses to be added of living, clothing, &c.; and lastly, but not least, we have the initial cost of land.

It should be noted that in "the jungles" there are rarely concise and definite boundaries, consequently more land is taken up than is ever cultivated, or even cultivatable. Rupees 50 and 100 are by no means rare prices for land as we have seen. In the Wynaad, little can be got under Rs. 30 per acre. But if we give as little as Rs. 5, this will be on, perhaps, 400 acres—Rs. 2,000. Very cheap land—and very inconvenient—with poor transport facilities and a scanty labour market, is always dear at any price, unless the soil is so genuinely good that it must be well and quickly patronized, and thus civilization overtake the pioneer in the midst of his struggles. It is wiser for a young man to purchase a small holding, one well covered by the limits of his capital, say allotting £20 to every acre he is going to open in three years, than to burden himself with wide, barren domains, where his money will be absorbed like water on the desert sands, and with as little result. The same thing applies to companies, who are likely to get a good dividend much sooner and much more regularly by the thorough and skilful cultivation of a moderate extent of well-planted land than by rushing recklessly forward presumably with the idea that profits depend on the "paper" acreage under Coffee in their names.

"Forty times out of fifty," an old planter says, "the true reason of failure and disappointment in this branch of agriculture is due to more land being taken in hand than the limits of available capital warrant." Borrowing does not do in India or elsewhere, and there it is especially ruinous since money cannot be got under 9 or 10 per cent. We know it has been said land can be brought into bearing for £8 and £10 an acre. Undoubtedly it can, in a manner, but in a style neither cheap nor profitable, and which means constant patching and mending with means which might be turned to much better account. The Englishman who is misled by such statements, and plunges into Coffee planting "with 'Young Ceylon' in one pocket and £1,000 in the other" will speedily find he has been over-confident. Still £1,000 is a handsome "nest egg," and to the possessor of such we would say, by advertising or through friends get a berth as assistant on a garden in Southern India, Fiji, or anywhere else, and serve three years' apprenticeship. During those three years learn everything you can, important or trivial, and not forgetting the local language. By the end of that time you will be well qualified to judge of whether it is safe to invest your capital in forest, whether it would not be wiser to take over a half-opened garden from a discontented neighbour, or to throw in your lot with some pleasant and clever "chum," and make your fortunes over a joint estate.

"The first year a learner has a house on the estate but no pay; the second year they usually get Rs. 100 a-month pay (profits of course, too, if a partner); and after that Rs. 150, with a bonus on crop over a certain quantity. As far as my own experience goes, it is easier to get a berth *whilst still in England* than when actually on the spot. Advertising, as we know it at home, is unknown abroad, and unless he has plenty of friends, the adventurer who goes out on the chance of something to do *to India or Ceylon* will find himself hopelessly stranded. In younger countries he will have a slightly better lookout."

Profits are a vague but pleasant subject, the outcome and dependent of all we have written. One planter appealed to on this subject shakes his head gloomily and declares there are *none*. Another, with whom we agree, takes, in the columns of the *Field*, a more hopeful view:—

"People say Coffee does not pay to cultivate, and upon the face of it there is much in support of this contention; but it would not be difficult to show that Coffee has been made to pay, and pay well, and that under circumstances as adverse, or even more adverse, than those existing at the present moment. Twenty years ago a planter considered himself a fortunate man if he got thirty rupees per cwt. for his Coffee on the coast; now he would consider himself very unfortunate in having to accept that price. Yet to-day the cost of labour is not greater, while carriage to and from the coast is less. Coffee paid then, why should it not pay now? The answer is not far to seek, strange though at first sight that answer may appear to be. I say advisedly, the high prices that were experienced some few years ago, and which led to a large area of land being planted which under no condition was suitable for the cultivation of Coffee. Something also must be put down to reckless expenditure—the child of temporary prosperity. But what about leaf disease? I do not believe that to Coffee cultivated under conditions not inimical to its growth it will do any material injury, however fatal it may have been to the class of estates referred to above, and worn out properties, of which there are many such in every district. As is the case in all epidemics, the aged and the infirm are the sufferers. Taking the most adverse view of Coffee, it is no worse than it was twenty years ago, when it was considered a good investment, while its prospects in the future are for many reasons brighter. The low price of Coffee in 1860 tended to restrict production, which, reacting on value, led to the high rate realised in 1873. This stimulating production has brought about the present state of the Coffee market. As it has been in the past, will it not be in the future? Have we not evidence of this already in Ceylon and elsewhere? Old and worthless estates are being abandoned, while new plantations are seldom or never heard of, and this leads to a limitation in production, to be followed hereafter by enhanced value of the article."

Profits depend on two things chiefly—the selling price of clean Coffee, and the weight yielded per acre; quality, we are sorry to say, has not much to do with the matter.

Suppose expenses of working an established garden, including manager allowances, overseers pay, &c., are put at Rs. 100 per acre per annum; then with an average yield, Coffee at £94 per ton, and no untoward circumstances, we should be making something like 15 per cent. on money invested. But suppose Coffee went down to £64 a ton, profits would give way in proportion, and if we had spent £60 per ton, including all charges, in *growing* the crop it will be seen the margin would be decidedly narrow. The planter, like any other merchant, desires to obtain cheap and sell dear. A combination of evils is arrived at when there is over much clean Coffee in the markets, when prices drop steadily, and added to this "leaf disease" and other ills curtail private production.

1. A yield under 3 cwt. per acre,
2. A selling price under £60 per ton,
3. And interest to pay at the rate of 10 per cent. on a heavy debt,

are the black clouds of the planter's sky; on the other side—

1. A yield over the average 5 cwt. per acre,
2. A selling price nearer £80 than £60,
3. And last, but not least, some free working capital at the bankers,

form a bright look-out on the horizon, a ready road to fortune, and thus to that return to the native country which is the goal of even the most contented Anglo-Indian.

Certain estates in Ceylon for a long time gave an average yield of 9½ cwt. a year at times when the market was very high. No wonder the prosperity of the island increased as these properties and others like them drew wealth and commerce to her shores.

Very many estates in the best times of the enterprise returned regularly 30 and 40 per cent. on their opening costs, and fortunes were made rapidly. Then came the leaf disease, and "bug," and now there can be no doubt but that the planters are discouraged. It by no means follows that Coffee in Ceylon or Southern India is played out. Restricted planting means (even in face of other producing countries) a smaller supply which in turn leads to an enhanced price. Not only so, but by our most recent news from the East, the leaf disease is showing signs of decreasing severity—passing over estates without doing a fraction of the damage it once did. Everything points to the fact that Coffee will flourish again, and even to-day, if we keep ourselves out of debt, and earn by careful cultivation some twelve or thirteen per cent. on the capital embarked, we shall have little cause to grumble, since there are very few branches of agriculture which yield any greater per centage with regularity. The life, too, if a hard one at first, is by no means without its pleasures — the noble scenery of the hills, the free existence, and the sense of honourable toil, combined with occasional holidays into the plains, a little sport now and then, and last but not least (let us hope) a prospect of increasing wealth, tend to elevate it into the region of a very pleasant labour.

CHAPTER XX.

COFFEE COUNTRIES.

BETWEEN well-recognised limits north and south of the Equator Coffee is found growing, and bearing highly-profitable crops, in a wide range of countries.

To attempt anything like an exhaustive account of these would be manifestly impossible within the range of a single chapter; but a few facts are given which will at least give a good general idea of the individual districts, and for more detailed information the planter must refer to local sources of information. In

BRITISH INDIA,

Coffee is grown along the summits and slopes of the Western Ghauts, from the northern limits of Mysore south to Cape Comorin; in Coorg, Travancore, in the Wynaad, on the slopes of the Neilgherry Hills, and also on the Shevaroy Hills and Pulney Hills. Major Bevan introduced Coffee into the Wynaad about the year 1822 as a curiosity; Mr. Cannon, somewhat later, formed a plantation in Mysore; Mr. Glasson, in 1840, started a plantation in Manautoddy; and in 1842 it was growing well at Belgaum. The extension since has been great. In 1880, in the Cochin, Travancore, Mysore, and Madras districts, and at Lohardugga in Bengal, 412,947 acres had been taken up for Coffee, of which 162,847 acres had mature plants.

Java and Sumatra

Claim our attention first. Java Coffee sells at 45s. when best Ceylon plantation is fetching 80s., but this only points to the fact that much Coffee from thence is poorly dried, and comes over "country damaged," &c. The soil of the island is good enough to produce as fine a sample as was ever grown. Land does not seem to be difficult to procure.

Any foreigner residing in Java, and elsewhere in Netherlands India, may apply for and obtain, under the same rules and regulations applicable to the Dutch themselves, Government waste lands. They can purchase and become possessors of Government contracts running for seventy-five years from their original holders. The size of most of these contracts is 500 bouws—one bouw = $1\frac{2}{3}$ acre—and quit rent varies from 6 dols. to 20 dols. per bouw per annum, payable on the sixth year from time of purchase, the average amount being at 9 dols. per bouw. The purchase sum for such contract varies, but if the site and soil be good, 50 dols. per bouw, roughly speaking £7 per acre, is not considered out of the way, and this is by far the pleasanter and more practicable way of acquiring land for Coffee or

Cinchona, as delays in the instance of applying to Government for waste land are endless and very vexatious.

Trees are planted out usually 7 by 8 feet apart, *i.e.*, 780 to the acre. The "dadap" is the favourite shade tree, while the planters have a curious plan of letting the grass grow tall and strong between the rows until their Coffee is established. At two years old bushes flower and bear.

The "voor pluk" begins in February, the "main pluk" in May or June. This is the "full pluk," when the heavy portion of the crop is gathered. The "after pluk" is a general sweep of fallen seed. Plucking must be got through in two months. The yield is an average of from three quarters of a pound to one and a quarter pounds of clean Coffee per bush. Much of the seed is "hulled"—*i.e.*, dried as a cherry on the drying grounds, the brittle pulp after fifteen days or a month's exposure being knocked off in a special machine.

The cost of plucking varies, but may be set down at 2 rupees (1s. 8d.) per picul of 136 lbs. of clean Coffee. Six piculs of red berry equal 1 picul of clean Coffee.

The wages for cultivation are very trifling. There is a teeming population of workers in Java, and, as a consequence, wages are almost nominal. The style of payment in vogue in Java is to give a man a bit of rice ground, on which he grows his own food, together with about 30 to 50 cents more or less per day. The plantation hands live contentedly on this—what would appear to us—miserable pittance. Coffee, like every other product which is dependent upon atmospheric phenomena for its success, varies in different seasons. The very best yield ever known in Java was 13 piculs of clean Coffee per bahoe, or 1,768 lbs. English, equal to about 867¾ lbs. per acre. An average yield is from 3 to 9 piculs of clean Coffee per bahoe. But then rises the dread form of the leaf disease, and by the latest accounts this is showing itself strongly. From an authoritative source we hear it was inevitable that the fell fungus should run its destructive course, lava soil to the contrary, and now it seems but a question of time for Coffee to be as great a failure in Java as it has turned out to be in Ceylon. The latest accounts are most serious, thus :—*Batavia.*—From the Director of Inland Administration information has been received that the coffee-leaf disease is becoming more and more noticeable in East Java, chiefly in the provinces of Pasaruan, Probolinggo, and Bezukie, which hitherto had been exempt from this infliction. The Coffee trees there abound in berries everywhere, but owing to the disease all the leaves have dropped off. In many estates the trees display nothing else but branches full of berries, which are still fresh-looking and green, but have become partially black and have dropped off. As the disease shows itself everywhere, in mid Java also, where it is widespread in the province of Bagelen, it is to be feared that the Coffee yield will fall off in consequence more than ever.

Sumatra is under the same rule as Java, and shares for the most part its good and bad characteristics, though it has never made itself quite such a home of the shrub as the delightful and beautiful sister island. No other Coffee acquires, except by artificial means, the dark yellowish-brown shade that marks the Java and Sumatra bean, which colour governs, in a great measure, its commercial value. Another very good indication of genuineness is the size of the bean, which is considerably larger than that of other kinds of Coffee, excepting Liberian. There is, however, some Coffee produced in the other islands of the Malay Archipelago which does not differ materially in size of bean or general appearance, but which, as a rule, is inferior in flavour.

The Java and Dutch India crops of 1885 are calculated to be 8,000 tons less than those produced in the previous year.

Fiji

"Is not a country for the white man," said Sir Arthur Gordon; but, as usual, the white man is loath to admit it, and the island is being slowly opened by enterprise and spirit in the face of many difficulties.

There can be no question but that Fiji possesses an abundant store—almost limitless, in fact—of the best volcanic land for Coffee cultivation, which has been successfully established, and largely increased since the British annexation in 1874. The labour question is a serious one, as it often is in new colonies. "Fiji was taken over to try and preserve the native races, and Government think that if they were allowed to do as they liked they would die out. Therefore they are induced to stay at home as much as possible and keep themselves to themselves, to cultivate Government gardens only to enable them to pay taxes," says A. J. S., writing to the *Ceylon Observer*. The planters in the new colony complain of the "grandmotherly" care exercised by the authorities over natives, and how the latter make planters' lives a burthen to them by continually taking cases to court which in other countries would be considered beneath notice. The above writer declares he was summoned for calling a coolie "a b—— fool," and, objectionable as the language may have been, it illustrates the sort of "complaints" which the natives hatch and support by false testimony.

Nor is the supply of Polynesian labour sufficient or as good as it once was.

"The Government in 1883 only succeeded in getting one vessel to recruit Polynesians, and the estimated cost was £16 per head. The vessel was unsuccessful, the men have been given out at £30 per head to those planters who cared about giving such a figure. In 1878 and 1879 men used to be £9, including depôt expenses. The men also are not of so good stamp as they once were—mere boys and old men are allowed to come." This drives the planters back upon Indian labourers.

It seems quite certain that, as yet, Coffee has not been an assured success in Fiji. *Hemeleia vastatrix* may not be so virulent as it has proved to be in Ceylon, but the wet climate has developed another bad blight in the shape of " black leaf." Such Coffee as is grown, too, is not well cured, although the single curing mill erected is but poorly patronised. Last season in Fiji seems to have been worse for excessive rainfall than even that of 1882 in Ceylon. From a rainfall of 110 in., the quantity went up to 183 in., an increase of 73 in one year; and it will be observed from the monthly returns that as nearly as possible 100 in. fell in the four months, December to March. No wonder, although the Coffee blossoms were destroyed. Of course, it would not be logical to judge the Coffee enterprise by the results of one year; but we have now the experience of a good many years before us, and we have a right to say that the prospects of Coffee in Fiji are not all that could be wished.

From Messrs. Gordon and Gotch's "Australian Handbook for 1885" we glean the following information :—

Since 15th March, 1877 (the date the "Real Property" Ordinance came into operation), 1,020 deeds have been issued, conveying 312,400 acres of land, consideration given for the same amounting to £25,477.

CLIMATE.—The climate of Fiji as a whole is most agreeable and healthy; and, considering its proximity to the Equator, is not nearly so hot as might be expected, the fierceness of the sun's heat being lessened by sea breezes. For nine months in the year the climate is delightful and free from diseases, though during the hot season dysentery is prevalent. The mean temperature of the colony is about 80°, the greatest extremes being experienced inland. 60° is the lowest and 122° the highest hitherto noted. From Christmas to March is called the hurricane season, but there has been no heavy blow since 1879. There is a dry and a wet season; the former is cool and lasts from May to October, the latter is hot and lasts from October to May. The meteorological observations taken during 1880 at Delanasau Bay (S. lat. 16° 38', E. long. 178° 37') by Mr. Holmes were as follows:—Barometer 29.893, thermometer, highest reading 93°, lowest 59°, mean 78° 9'. Rainfall on 168 days, amount 115.61 inches; greatest daily fall 7.79 inches. On the Ra Coast, according to Mr. Leefe, rain fell on 135 days, the total rainfall being 102.63 inches.

NATIVES.—The Fijian aborigines are a handsome, powerful-looking set of people; a dark copper is their principal colour; they are said to be a cowardly, unprincipled race, lazy and tricky, but with a little management the white man can make them subserviently useful. They are cleanly in their persons, in fact so fond of the water that they are (both male and female) semi-amphibious.

LABOUR.—The importation of foreign labour from the New Hebrides, Solomon, and other Polynesian islands has of late become a self-sustaining institution of the colony. Eighteen vessels, with an aggregate of about 3,000 tons, are engaged during the season in conveying upwards of 2,000 persons. Still the supply is not equal to the demand. Government supervises the whole matter of labour, from the time the vessel goes for them, during the term—three years—of engagement in Fiji, until their return home.

Of the cost per head to the planter of these labourers no statistics have been published, but, approximately, it is £16 per annum—viz., one-third of indent for three years, £3; wages, £3; food, £4 15s; return home, £4; landing at plantation, 2s. 6d.; quarters, 10s.; mats, 5s.; blankets, 8s.; sulus, 10s.; medicine and proprietor of hospital house, 10s.

The cost of Fijian labour is about £17, and of coolie £19. Size of house, bedding, clothing, stock of medicines, daily rations, periodical inspections are all laid down by ordinance. On return home these labourers receive presents of axes, tomahawks, beads, &c., but not muskets as formerly. In 1883 a new law came into force, which will have the effect of increasing the cost about 15 per cent., as well as, from its stringency, drive small capitalists from their fields of labour. Just as the labourer is becoming most useful to his employer the time expires, and he is not allowed, even if he wishes it, to enter upon a new agreement for more than one year. Last year the allotment fee was £16, depôt fee £1, sundries about 5s. Government impedes the engagement of the natives as agricultural labourers for more than one month at a time, even though they desire; and foreign labour is scarce, which is ever the case upon an influx of capital. It is very probable that before long coolie labour will exclude Polynesian.

COOLIES.—In 1879 the authorities arranged with the Indian Government for the introduction of coolie labour. The second and third attempts made in 1883 and 1884 have proved very successful. By a late ordinance, for every coolie applied for £6 *per caput* has to be paid in advance to the Government.

CROWN LANDS.—At Suva these are sold by auction at a high upset price per acre, one half down, the other moiety in three months. Improvements to be effected to twice the amount of the price within two years if less than upset price; if more, within five years. On default, the Government resume possession and return two-thirds of the purchase-money. Crown surveyor values and disputes are settled by arbitration.

COFFEE was first exported from Fiji in 1877, and although the amount was under £200, yet, as several of the most wealthy and enterprising planters are now engaged in its cultivation, Coffee is rapidly becoming one of the chief exports of the island. Average yield 4 to 5 cwt. per acre. The leaf disease which threatened the Coffee in 1880 and 1881 is said to have decreased, at least for the time.

Year.	Total Exports.	Value.
	lbs.	£ s. d.
1881	104,524	4,666 5 0
1882	62,328	2,782 10 0
1883	210,204	9,383 19 7

The quantity of Coffee exported will no doubt increase in future years.

A good overseer or sub-manager gets from £150 to £250 now, managers from £300 to £400, or perhaps more; but billets like these are very scarce.

BORNEO.

This island can grow good Coffee. A correspondent writes:—

"Sandakan, 14th Feb., 1884.

"Since the country was first started, some 200,000 acres of forest lands have been selected by Cantonese, European and Australian planters. Of this land, some 40,000 acres have now been surveyed in blocks varying in sizes of ¼ acre to 12,000 acres. In all about 1,000 acres have been cleared, and about 400 acres planted up. The gardens at Silam are, I hear, looking very encouraging, especially as regards 'new product.' A trial of cacao and Liberian Coffee on a small scale here, and planted in Ceylon style, is looking well, as also the few Liberian trees 'put in' by the Cantonese, whose estates, owing to having 'gone in for' extravagant cleaning-up (much beyond that which is usually done), will take a long time to pay. The place requires some Ceylon men to make it a success. With our splendid and well-proportioned rainfall, everything grows extremely well, especially cacao and Liberian Coffee, for which our soil and climate seem to be well suited. A great many of the clearings here owned by both Europeans and natives are managed by men who have scarcely ever seen jungle, and hold extraordinary ideas as to 'clearing-up' and weeding, and think as the Malays do: 'Man plants ("sticks in" it is appropriately called), and Providence looks after the seeds.' It is hoped that some of these people will soon see the error of their ways and obtain practical assistance.

"We are fairly well supplied with labour from Brunei, Labuan, Singapore and Hongkong for thirty dollar cents per day (which we hope to reduce); the coolies from the latter place are, however, 'at sea' in the jungle or on plantations, and consequently not much use, but may perhaps, like their employers, with the aid of practical assistance and advice, become better in time."

New Guinea

Must fall into European hands sooner or later, and no hands are so fit for it to fall into as ours. Under English rule it might become the garden of the Pacific; under a German flag it will be a constant thorn in the side of Anglo-Saxon Australasia.

The *Argus* special correspondent, Capt. Armit,

in his latest letter, dated Wabadam, July 27th, 1884, has the following:—

"I inspected the gardens, and was astonished at the luxuriance of the crops, 1,550 feet above sea level. The people of this country have no conception of the capabilities of the soil. The natives grow more than they want, and this suffices. Were these lands in the hands of European planters we should soon be astonished at their productiveness. Coffee, cinchona, cocoa, ginger, vanilla, rice (mountain), and a host of fruit trees could be admirably grown here. Ceylon has been almost ruined by the Coffee leaf-disease (*Hemilia vastatrix*), and many planters have been inquiring in Queensland for land suitable for Coffee growing. Here they will find not only land of the best quality, but also labour at their very doors. If these people are kindly and honestly treated they will work, and work willingly and well for the Britaniata, as they call us. But England must take the utmost care that, in purchasing the land, the present proprietors receive a fair value for it. If, after a few years, they find out that they have been swindled, there will be serious trouble. They will soon obtain firearms and learn how to use them. Then they will not prove contemptible foes, especially as they have quite sense enough to join together and make common cause. I do not desire to dishearten intending settlers, but everyone should know what the people are like, and that in coming to New Guinea they will find an agricultural race owning the soil, and perfectly aware that they do own it—not a race of unfortunates like the Australians, who, after being robbed of their land, were left to perish of starvation, or ruthlessly shot down for daring to hunt over their own soil.

"Cane 16 ft. high, Bourbon ribbon, and, I believe, Scott's cane or Otaheite, a small yellow sort; bananas in full bearing, the large bunches tied up in leaves; bread-fruit trees (*Artocarpus incisa*) 50 ft. high, and plantations of small trees of all sizes; taro, whappa, a very large-leaved species of arum, yams, sweet potatoes, tobacco, pumpkin—all were growing here in profusion. The tillage also is superior to anything of the kind

I have yet seen in the island. The weeds are kept down, and the soil well and deeply worked. In clearing the land, the graceful palms have been spared, and add an element of beauty to the scene as they raise their graceful fronds 70 ft. to 100 ft. above the plantations. The country to the south of Wabadam is open forest with isolated hills and ridges strewn over its surface. The natives do not cultivate their flats. The soil is too hard, and would require heavy labour before it could be utilized. The scrub soil, on the contrary, is always moist and loose. It is easily worked after the scrub has been cleared, and remains light and friable."

There is a great future before New Guinea, and the earliest settlers will reap the richest harvest!

BURMAH.

A very large portion of the surface of British Burmah, admirably adapted for various kinds of cultivation, still remains in its primeval state of unproductive jungle. This is due to the entire absence of natural energy on the part of the Burmese, who have been described as the idlest race under the sun—presenting in this respect a singular contrast to their active and industrious brethren of the Celestial Empire. The total area of old British Burmah is 87,220 square miles, and according to the last Administration Report, only 5,498 square miles are under cultivation, of which about 88 per cent. are devoted to the production of rice. Labour has been as scarce as in a dozen other localities of like nature. The immigration question is one which for long engaged the attention of the local authorities, and we learn that a definite arrangement—proposed some time back—has at length been entered into with the British India and the Asiatic Steam Navigation Companies regarding the fares of deck passengers between the East Coast of India and Rangoon. According to agreement these companies are to carry deck passengers to Rangoon from Calcutta for Rs. 5 a-head; from any of the ports north of Madras for Rs. 8; and from Madras, or any of the ports south of it, for Rs. 10 a-head. The Government undertakes to supplement these charges by a grant of Rs. $\frac{1}{8}$ for each passenger from Calcutta, and Rs. $\frac{2}{8}$ for each passenger from other ports. It is probable that the reduction of fares will have the effect of inducing a considerable number of stout-limbed coolies to listen to the voice of the coolie-maistry, and try their fortune on the other side of the *kala pani*. The coolie-maistry engages labourers at one of the coast ports, pays their passage over to Burmah, keeps them in a barrack there, and hires them out till they have repaid all expenses incurred in their behalf, with a handsome *douceur* to the enterprising maistry in addition. Labour of every description is very dear in Burmah.

A bid is now being made for the presence of men who understand the art of planting Tea,

Coffee, and spices. Such men are offered (by reiterated advertisements) free grants of jungle land in the Tavoy district, in a tract lying between the 13° and 14° parallel of north latitude. The lots placed at altitudes ranging from 100 to 6,800 feet above the level of the sea, and exposed to a rainfall of about 200 inches, vary in size from 100 to 1,200 acres. The only immediate payment required is 8 annas per acre for cost of survey and demarkation. The grantee will not be called upon to pay any land revenue till the tenth year of possession, when he will be taxed at the rate of Rs. 1 4 annas an acre. He is welcome to every stick of timber he finds on his lot, but the Government reserve to themselves all possible minerals which may exist underground, with due compensation for any damage caused to the grantee's land by search or mining operations. To encourage pioneers in the Coffee and Cinchona enterprise in Tavoy, Government promised to "pay to the first four grantees who began *bonâ fide* planting operations Rs. 15 per head for every Indian or Chinese coolie, male or female, over sixteen years of age, who may be settled and housed on their plantations before the 1st of March, 1885." One of the advantages of the district is that steamers to and from Rangoon touch weekly at a port in the district. The Chief Commissioner seems to be very anxious to establish

Cinchona plantations in the province, for a reward of Rs. 100 has been offered to any Karen who will undertake Cinchona cultivation; but as yet no application has been made for any of the plants. Every explanation of the above plan of settlement will be afforded on application to the Deputy Commissioner of Tavoy, the Commissioner of Tenasserim at Moulmein, or the Secretariat, Rangoon. The subject is worth the attention of young planters with a little ready cash on hand.

How the district will prosper remains to be seen, but those on the spot are sending home rosy accounts of the new land. It is one in which labour should become abundant, where soil should be cheap and good, "leaf disease" absent or nearly so, and in a country presenting exceptional chances and openings to a young man, while the climate on the hills is said to be very healthy. "People seem to have little knowledge of where Tavoy is; their geographical knowledge regarding British Burma is only limited: one man thinks it's awfully moist and unhealthy, and another wants to know if the land is still under King Theebaw! The climate is similar to Ceylon and healthy for Europeans in the extreme; they all get fat. The rainfall this year, 190 inches. The rain commences showery in April and May. In June the monsoon sets in, and breaks up in July, the end of; then from July to middle of November nice showers; no rain from middle of November to middle of February; then a few nice showers only; also a few showers in March, a heavy dew at night, just the thing for the young planties. The blossom season same as in Ceylon : January, February and March, blossom in all the jungle, and also Coffee and all fruit-bearing trees, durian, mangosteen, caju-nuts, &c., &c.; and as for 'King Theebaw,' he is farther away than the old home."

Samoa.

Regarding this fertile little territory the *Indian Mercury* says :—

"An interesting official report has been published concerning the resources of Samoa (Navigators' Island), and we note that experts both for sugar and Coffee planting have favourably reported upon the capabilities of the islands for these industries. The Coffee plant has been in existence there for some years, and, growing luxuriantly, has proved the suitability of the climate and soil, but it has never been scientifically treated, and in consequence is not as yet an article of commerce. Some Coffee planters and speculators visited Samoa during the past year with the view of settling, should they find the country suitable for their several purposes; but the moral impossibility, under the present circumstances, of obtaining an indisputable title to any parcel of land they might buy deterred them from risking their capital. The native tenure of land is intricate and complicated, and the inclination of the natives to effect wrongful sales, with a view of reclaiming the land subsequently, makes speculators very chary of investing money in property that may at any time be disputed, perhaps at one time on account of neglect of some native custom not noticed at time of sale, and not provided against ; and perhaps at another time by some relative presenting himself, who was absent at the time of sale, either intentionally or accidentally, and questioning the validity of sale on account of his not having given his consent, and having received no part of the purchase-money. The total absence of hurricanes, or indeed of any winds strong enough to cause damage, make these islands more suitable for the growth of sugar-cane than many other parts of the world, where the whole crop is liable to be destroyed in one blow. In starting a plantation in Samoa, after acquiring the land, the greatest difficulty would be in procuring labour. The supply of Polynesian labourers is visibly falling off, through the disinclination of natives to go to Samoa to work, and the greater advantages and comfort offered them in other parts, such as Queensland and Fiji."

A Ceylon planter who has made a personal visit to the island takes a rather more cheerful view. Doubtless here as elsewhere some men will succeed while others will fail from the very first. He writes:—

"Of Coffee there were a few trees planted at an elevation of about 500 to 600 feet above sea-level and looked remarkably well. There was no leaf disease or other pest that I noticed. A Coffee planter has opened a nursery of some 600,000 seedlings, which were to be planted out and, I believe, will do very well indeed. The soil is a chocolate loam of great depth. Labour, however, is the great drawback. They have to get all their coolies from the Hebrides and Solomon Islands, which are a long way off, and are also the recruiting ground for the Fiji and Queensland planters, so that Samoa is pretty well handicapped in this respect.

"The land is all mountainous, but does not rise abruptly from the sea. Towards the beach it is planted with cocoanut groves, throughout which are innumerable villages. Coral reefs circle all the islands, inside which the water is smooth and rarely ruffled by anything but a gentle breeze. To say they are inviting, enchanting and altogether charming does no more than express the feelings of all visitors. I was pleased and delighted beyond telling with my stay.

"Darwin's sentence applies with truth here: 'Every

form, every shade of Nature so completely surpasses in magnificence all that the European has ever beheld in his own country that he knows not how to express his feelings.'"

"SINGAPORE JAVA.

"This is Coffee shipped from the English free port of that name. Singapore is situated on a small island, eight or ten miles square, and not of itself particularly fertile; yet this place is the great emporium for the productions of the whole Malayan Peninsula and Archipelago, comprising hundreds of islands, many of them of large size, and upon which many valuable and important articles are produced.

"The exports from Singapore were, according to the Singapore market report, as follows :—

To GREAT BRITAIN.		
Year.	Piculs.	Pounds.
1875	16,827	2,288,472
1876	20,292	2,759,712
1877	16,115	2,191,640
1878	8,379	1,139,544
1879	16,462	2,238,832
1880	19,948	2,712,928

To UNITED STATES.		
Year.	Piculs.	Pounds.
1875	16,588	2,255,968
1876	13,947	1,896,792
1877	5,452	741,472
1878	9,248	1,257,728
1879	22,324	3,036,064
1880	6,277	853,672

"The Coffee exported from Singapore is raised in the small islands of Netherlands India, and the Philippine Islands. It does not possess the fine flavour and intrinsic value of Padang and Batavia Java, and some years it is of decidedly inferior quality. All Java Coffee received here, and which was produced free from the restrictions imposed by the Government, is known as 'Free Coffee.'"—*Coffee, from Plantation to Cup*, F. B. THURBER.

THE PHILIPPINES

Are said to be peculiarly adapted to the raising of Coffee, and we can well believe it. The berry produced is equal if not superior in aroma and flavour to that of Java, under which name it often finds its way with much other island-grown Coffee to Singapore (as above stated), and so to Europe or the United States.

Most of the small annual crop, which does not exceed 3,300 tons per annum, is native grown, but there are a few lonely European planters dotted about the Archipelago.

AUSTRALIA.

Here, too, they have tried Coffee culture, but we cannot say we think it is likely to be profitable when grown on a large scale, in spite of Mr. Pink. From Queensland Mr. Pink writes:—

"I think there is no advantage in growing *Coffea Liberica* here at present, as the leaf disease is unknown, and *Coffea Arabica* does well, producing at the rate of 6 cwt. per acre. There are now in this colony a number of Coffee planters from Ceylon who are anxious to go into Coffee growing here, and the Minister of Lands is about to have a quantity of suitable land reserved for that purpose. The small farmers are likewise just discovering that Coffee pays better than corn and potatoes when there is a family of children to pick the berries. Several farmers have brought and sold to the merchants of Brisbane green Coffee berries at the rate of 10d. per lb. this season. Consequently the demand for plants has become very great, but fortunately we have an equally large supply on hand to meet it, both of *Liberica* and *Arabica*. The great fear—we may say the absolute certainty—is that leaf-disease, which exists in Ceylon, in Mauritius and Fiji, will sooner or later affect Coffee grown in Queensland."

This does not exhaust the possible spots in the Pacific where Coffee may be tried with great advantage, but touches upon some chief centres of the planting enterprise.

South America,

From hence half the world has drawn supplies for a long time—indeed "Brazilian Coffee" is an expression bracketed with "Mocha Coffee" and "Ceylon Coffee" all over the civilized globe—chance or some happy common virtue of soil or climate having given the produce of these favoured spots especial fame.

Brazil.

The following is the picture which the author of "Wanderings South and East" gives us of Brazil:—

"Coffee, Coffee everywhere: whole forests cleared away to make place for Coffee—whole hills close shorn for Coffee; Coffee above on the right and again below on the left; Coffee along the valleys and along the hill-brows, and down the slopes and up the rise; Coffee drying in the sun on flat open floors in front of peasants' houses; Coffee in piles near the cottage doors, or in sacks ready for carting; waggon-loads of Coffee being drawn toilfully along towards the railway; Coffee, too, in little cups on the counters of wayside inns— in fact, everywhere Coffee. It is deplorable to see the awful destruction of vegetable life in the production of this berry. The virgin forest is burnt, and the hill-side disfigured with smouldering logs and stumps. The lovely valleys are stripped clean, and Coffee reigns supreme over hill and dale. Agassiz convinced himself that this rich country had been swept by glacial action, and that most successful Coffee plantations were found exactly where the movements of ice had most enriched the soil by transportation and mixture of its combined elements. Half the entire supply of the world comes from these hills, which are said to produce no less than 260,000 tons per annum!"

The Brazilian climate varies greatly. As a rule the rainy season commences in June and lasts until November. The limits differ, however, according to locality. In June all vegetation ceases, all seeds ripen; in July the leaves commence to turn yellow and to fall; in August vast tracts of land present the aspect of a European winter without snow, with two or three exceptions the trees being denuded of leaves. Where the old mode of harvesting is in vogue, this is the most favourable season for the preparation of the Coffee cultivated on the mountains. Being gathered, it is spread on the ground, which exhales no moisture, but, on the contrary, absorbs it. Surrounded by an atmosphere in the same conditions, the Coffee dries rapidly without fermenting.

"From December to January the wet season sets in, and with the first rainfalls the rivers, which until then had been almost dry, with only here and there a few pools, which served as watering-places for cattle or as a refuge for fish, swell immensely. Plants in a few days, as by a charm, reacquire their verdancy; the soil is covered with parti-coloured flowers; alimentary plants grow quickly and produce abundantly."

"The Coffee of Brazil," says Mr. Thurber, whom we have quoted before, "varies greatly in colour and size. Most of the Rio Coffee received here is a small-sized bean, varying in colour from a light to a dark green, with some of a yellow hue, often denominated Golden Rio. Large quantities are artificially coloured, in order to meet the requirements of certain sections where a prejudice exists in favour of some peculiar colour. Various chemicals are used in the process, some of which are rank poison, while others are comparatively harmless. By simply washing in clear cold water it may easily be determined if the bean has been artificially coloured. The flavour of most of the Rio Coffee imported into the United States is, as has been before stated, quite marked and entirely different from that of any other sort. The planters generally forward their Coffee to a *commissario*, or factor, who acts as their agent. It is received in all sorts of lots and conditions from many different growers, no regularity being observed in the style of bag or the amount it contains. The factor sells his stock to the dealers or packers (*ensaccadores*), men that control large warehouses. Coffee culture extends from the Amazon to the province of San Paulo, and from the coast to the western limits of the empire—a surface exceeding 653,400 square kilometres. Within this territory it is estimated that there are about 530,000,000 Coffee trees, which cover an area of 1,400,000 acres. The Coffee plantations situated on the high lands, and exposed to the east, are the most productive, but the industry prospers even in the bottom lands, although the product is said to be inferior in flavour."

On the high lands the gathering of the crop begins in April or May and continues until November. The "West India process" of separating the pulp, and then washing and drying the seeds, prevails on most of the large estates.

Labour is a difficulty; many planters are said to have lately worked their estates to shreds, feeling certain that with the extinction of slave labour their chance of profit will be extinct. In fact, the general opinion seems to be, Coffee in Brazil has been overdone. "Recent reports estimate the stock of Coffee in Rio de Janeiro and Santos at no less than 815,000 bags—an enormous quantity, for which, of course, markets will have to be found. At the same time, many articles of ordinary food required for the consumption of the people, and which could easily be grown on the spot, continued to be largely imported, notably flour. We do not say that Brazil is poorer from having this large growth of Coffee—quite the contrary—but she would be both richer and more independent if much of her food was grown on the spot, for internal consumption; and that this should be the case with her new railways there can be no question. Brazil is suffering severely for having overdone Coffee cultivation and neglected the raising of food products needed by her people."

There does not seem to be any inducement for young Englishmen to establish themselves here while so much good soil under their own flag can be obtained. Not a little Brazilian Coffee is sold under the specious names of Laguara, Guatemala, Costa Rica, Martinique, &c.

Mexico.

From the Official English "Commercial Reports" we gather that the production of Coffee as an article of Mexican export may be said to have commenced within the past ten years. Previous to 1870 the imports of it into France and England were so insignificant as not to merit separate mention in the customs returns, and even in the United States, which has always taken by far the greater proportion of the crop, its sale at that time was comparatively small, about 1,800 to 2,700 cwt. How great an impetus has been given of late to this industry may be judged from the fact that in the year 1881 the imports into these three countries were: into England, 3,193 cwt.; France, 13,054 cwt.; and the United States, 124,213 cwt.; besides small amounts sent to Barcelona, Hamburg, Santander, and Antwerp.

The finest qualities of Coffee are produced on the western slopes of the Mexican plateau, in the States of Colima and Michoacan, but the supply is very little in excess of the home demand, and only a small quantity of these classes is exported. The great bulk of the Coffee that finds a market abroad is grown near Cordova and Orizaba, in the State of Vera Cruz, and also in the southern State of Oajaca. Up to a few years ago the berry used to be very carelessly prepared, and presented a bad appearance when offered for sale, which, added to the irregularity of the supply as also of the price, was probably the reason why it was not more extensively exported to Europe; but these defects are now being remedied, consequent on the establishment of a large and increasing trade, and it is probable that ere long Mexican Coffee will become better known and appreciated in the European markets.

New York price lists quote Mexican Coffee as follows:—

	Cents.
Cordova, green	9 to 10 per lb.
,, white	11 ,, 13 ,,
Oajaca, white	11 ,, 13 ,,

Liverpool prices were—

	s. s.
Mexican Coffee, good	52 to 62 per cwt.
,, ,, middling	44 ,, 49 ,,

A correspondent of the Galveston *News* gives some information regarding the territory of Soconusco, the possession of which is now a subject of dispute between Mexico and Guatemala:—

"It is a strip of land lying on the Pacific coast south-east of the Gulf of Tehuantepec, and extending from the Bay of Tonela to the Bay de Ocos, on the present line of Guatemala, a distance of about 200 miles, and reaching inland to the summit of the mountain range, from forty to fifty miles, containing about 8,000 square miles. It was celebrated before the Inquisition for its heavy yield of Coffee and fine quality of chocolate. On the Guatemalan side of the boundary these lands are held at very high prices. The valuable product of Coffee, chocolate, sugar, rice, cotton, vanilla and indigo is building up cities, beautifying the country, and enriching its commerce. Grant's Mexican Southern Railroad will penetrate this fertile region within two years. There is a perfect stampede for its possession. The invigorating temperature, pure water, mahogany, rosewood, walnut, Coffee, rice, sugar, &c., all combine to make it attractive. There are said to be single Coffee trees, ten or twelve years old yielding from twenty-five to fifty pounds of Coffee annually. Labour is cheap, and lands are sold to colonists by the Company on ten years' time, without interest."

OTHER AMERICAN STATES.

Venezuela and Colombia (where fine Coffee is grown between 4,000 and 6,000 feet above sea level) used to ship 7 to 12 per cent. of all Coffee consumed in the United States. Paraguay Coffee of the country is of an excellent quality, although its flavour is somewhat bitter. At present it is grown on a very limited scale, owing to the scarcity of capital, and to the length of time which is requisite before the cultivator is able to reap any benefit. It is calculated that on the average a period of five years or so must elapse before plantations are ripe for their first harvest. "In Costa Rica, they are grubbing up Coffee trees as being no longer profitable, and planting rubber instead, so Ceylon is not the only sufferer in Coffee."

The decadence of Coffee crops, generally, everywhere surely must eventually bring down the enormous stocks of Coffee, both in London and Europe.

Along the west coast of South America plantations are found, but only from the latter state is any quantity of beans exported.

Turning northwards, we have, in

British Honduras

A country with all the advantages of English rule. There would seem to be at present only one small Coffee estate in the colony, and that of an experimental character. The following description of this attempt will be read with interest, and it will be noticed that in this, as in all the more important industries, Mr. Morris (in " British Honduras," E. Stanford, Charing Cross) speaks of a regular supply of labour from external sources as essential to success :—

"About 100 acres had been cleared and established in Coffee under the shade of bananas, with corn as an intermediary crop. The Coffee trees—about 30,000—were from one to two years old, planted out. Seed had been obtained from Martinique, Trinidad and Guatemala. As a whole, the plantation was in a promising state; in some cases the trees were overshadowed by bananas, and consequently, the plants were weak and 'spindled.' There is no doubt also that the ground had been somewhat impoverished by the large crop of corn (maize) which was then being taken off.

"Most of the trees about two years old were, however, bearing their first crop, and looked as if, even at this early age, some two or three hundredweights per acre would be yielded by them. The plantation was well laid out, with roads and intervals of 18 feet dividing the blocks. Naturally, being a pioneering effort, the best mode of procedure adapted to the district could not be obtained at once; and, again, the difficulty of obtaining labour had hampered the undertaking and increased the expenses.

"I left the plantation, however, with a favourable impression respecting the possibility of growing good Coffee in

British Honduras, and I have no doubt that if coolie labour could be obtained, the whole of this western district would soon be dotted over with prosperous plantations. The cost of clearing and cleaning land ready for planting is put down at £6 per acre; the labourers, at present, owing to the remoteness of the district, get from 42 to 50 cents per day."

It is just this question of labour that is always arising. The *Times* observes :—

"It appears the high rate of wages which prevails on the Isthmus of Panama is attracting labour, and making the production of Coffee unprofitable in Costa Rica, Columbia, Venezuela, and even Brazil. Only in Spanish Honduras and British Guatemala can Coffee now be said to be profitable. The planters in Nicaragua, according to latest reports, have a difficulty in clearing their expenses. In countries farther south an annual loss is incurred, while in Brazil the shrinkage of the crop has attracted the serious attention of the Government. Wages have gone down in Honduras and Guatemala, and if the present depression in the price of Coffee continues, the Coffee planters of Brazil, Columbia, Venezuela, Costa Rica, and Nicaragua will be ruined, while the more fortunate planters of Mexico, Guatemala, and Honduras will have all they can do to hold their own. Notwithstanding this gloomy outlook, however, Coffee in Mexico is still believed to be the coming industry, because the railways running from the United States will bring the plantations into direct communication with the consumers. This advantage, together with fairly cheap labour, should prove decisive in the trade, supposing Mexico to have equal facilities with other Coffee-growing countries, such as Costa Rica, Ceylon, &c."

This brings us to the

WEST INDIES.

Of the lesser islands Dominica and Trinidad yield about 3,000 tons each, the rest of the group in the West Indies not producing enough to give them a position as first-class Coffee-growing countries. The total production of all the West India Islands does not exceed 40,000 to 42,000 tons. In regard to Dominica, Dr. Alford Nicholls reports on the rich-soiled, well-watered and heavily-timbered Layon Flats in this the largest of the Leeward Islands. He says the island is of volcanic origin, and some of its mountains rise to 5,000 feet. Dominica was once a scene of prosperous cultivation; but first the Maroon War (waged by escaped Negroes), then the effects of emancipation, and, finally, the destruction of the Coffee trees by an insect blight (*Cemeostoma coffeellum*) brought the island down to depths of depression. The blight still affects the Arabian Coffee, but, according to Dr. Nicholls, the Libèrian species resists its attacks. Cacao (so Dr. Nicholls spells it) flourishes even when neglected, and he mentions a red pottery clay eminently suitable for "claying" the beans. Were a road or a tramway run through the rich central flats, there would be a mine of wealth in the fine timbers alone, including the bullet tree (*Bumelia retusa*), the trunk of which sometimes attains a diameter of 7 feet, which means 21 in circumference! Also the green-heart (*Nectandra rodiœi*), which is placed first-class in Lloyd's list of timbers for shipbuilding.

During 1884 Coffee in Jamaica—the most important Coffee island of the region—was very fairly prosperous. In the previous year, 84,357 cwts. was exported, valued at £160,617, of which 51,153 cwts. went to the British Isles.

Of Liberian Coffee, 1,633 plants, and 17 qrs. of cherry for seed, were sent of the Government gardens—a very small amount.

During three years the number of acres under Coffee cultivation in the island has been —(1881) 19,885; (1882) 22,842; (1883) 21,132.

Ground provisions, which are the ordinary food of the people, occupy the largest cultivated acreage; next come the lands in sugar cane, and then those under Coffee.

Last year's mean rainfall is thus summarized in inches and fractions :—

Jan.	Feb.	March.	April.	May.	June.	Year.
4.50	2.35	3.39	3.35	8.45	4.92	
July.	Aug.	Sept.	Oct.	Nov.	Dec.	66.64
4.23	6.75	6.76	9.65	6.69	5.70	

In the district of the Santa Cruz Mountains the Coffee is grown upon the red ferruginous earth overlaying the white limestone formation. The climate and rainfall there is said to be very similar to those of Algiers.

In 1878-79 the area in Jamaica devoted to Coffee-growing was 22,853 acres. The following interesting facts respecting Jamaica Coffee are taken from a letter written by Mr. D. Morris to the *Ceylon Observer*, from the Botanical Department, Jamaica, in June, 1880. This gentleman says:—

"The crop of last season was sold, in some instances, at 130s. per cwt. I had the pleasure, the other day, of visiting Radnor plantation. I found it a good type of Jamaica estates, most of which have been in cultivation for more than a century and a-half. In some places the trees were poor and 'sticky,' but wherever the soil has been preserved, and especially in 'bosoms,' the trees were looking healthy and strong. In spite of 'no manure,' in spite of 'mammoty' weeding for generations, these trees were bearing good crops, and, moreover, the producer is able to obtain prices which Ceylon planters must envy.

"Owing to the large areas nominally included under one estate, the different 'Coffee-fields' are sometimes two or three miles away from the works, lying in 'bosoms' of the hills, and only visited for the occasional 'hoeing' and picking of the crop. Out of a nominal acreage of 1,000 acres often there are only 160 to 200 acres, and sometimes only about 60 or 80 acres, under cultivation. The other parts are in 'reccinate' (jungle), or so steep that owing to 'breakaways' and rocks it is impossible to cultivate them. This gives a Jamaica Coffee estate a very patchy appearance, and as cinchona has not yet been taken up generally by planters, the uncultivated areas greatly exceed those cultivated. Much more might be done with the suitable Coffee lands if a regular system of nurseries were established and plants put out with greater care. At present new lands are planted up with 'suckers' (or rather seedlings) found under the trees. These are pulled up with little or no care, even when they have six or eight primaries, and after being carried in bundles on heads exposed to the full rays of the sun, are put in holes and allowed to take their chance without shade or shelter.

"As far as I have noticed, there is little disease on any of the cultivated plants of Jamaica. With the exception of the *Cemiostoma coffeeilum,* a little leaf miner similar to the *Gracilaria coffeefoliella* (Nietner) of Ceylon, which cause the silvery tortuous markings and blotches on Coffee-leaves, Jamaica Coffee appears to be very free from disease. Our old friend the black bug is here, but it does not give annoyance except sometimes to badly cultivated and young Coffee."

Yet this year he speaks discouragingly of Jamaica prospects. He mentions how, owing to the prevalence of comparative drought in the island for the last four years, Coffee in Manchester and in the lower hills, where settlers grow it, has suffered very severely. There is consequently a serious falling-off in the exports. While in 1883 there were exported 84,358 cwts. of Coffee of the value of £160,618, in 1884 the exports were only 48,378 cwts. of the value of £98,842. This is in quantity less than in any year since 1869. The Coffee industry will no doubt improve its position with the return of favourable seasons; but I fear, owing to the low prices which have been ruling for some years in this article, the settlers are gradually relinquishing the cultivation, and where fields are partially worn out, as in many districts of Manchester, they are being entirely abandoned.

Seventy-five years after the introduction of Coffee into Hayti the island exported nearly eighty millions of pounds per annum.

"The growers, however, exercised no care in handling it, and sent it to market ungraded and uncleaned, and demand in consequence gradually fell off. Owing to the enormously increasing production of Rio, its place was easily filled by this cheap Coffee, and those consumers who preferred a mild Coffee could obtain Maracaibos, Savanillas and Bogotas, though at higher prices. While the trade with the United States in this Coffee fell off, that with Europe increased, and it is one of the principal Coffees used in France and Germany, people there not being so exacting as regards grading and cleaning as are Americans. These shipments are made direct from Hayti to Europe, and also by way of New York, where sometimes a cargo finds a purchaser, the Coffee being very well adapted for mixing with Maracaibos and Javas. This was, in fact, one of its principal uses, when imported extensively into this country. The Coffee itself has a mild, pleasant flavour, which, with its cheapness, would commend it to many Coffee drinkers if it were properly cleaned and graded. A firm in this city, prominent in the West India trade, and which shipped large quantities of the Coffee to Europe, resolved to try the experiment of cleaning and grading it for the American market. The experiment proved a success, though there is considerable waste in cleaning."—*Rio News.*

In fact, of South America and the West Indies it may be said broadly that Nature does everything she can for Coffee, and man does as little as possible.

Eastwards, again, over the broad barrier of the Atlantic, we may note in passing that on St. Helena Coffee is grown in small patches varying from one-fourth of an acre to two or three acres. At Plantation House, Terrace Knoll, Bambu Groove, Elliotts,

Prospect, and Oaklands, fine patches of Coffee, somewhat neglected and unpruned, it is true, indicate the capabilities of the island to grow, in sheltered hollows, a fair quantity of very good Coffee. The extent of land actually suitable for Coffee is, however, small.

A lady traveller has spoken enthusiastically of the appearance of some shrubs planted in the Canary Islands, and a plantation has been established by a landowner in the neighbourhood of Rome. It is stated that he realized a fair profit with this year's harvest, which consisted of two tons of Coffee per hectare; but such facts are hardly more than curiosities, we fancy.

Africa,

However, is the real home of the plant, where it has always been indigenous, and Caffra, the district whence it takes its universal name, was but the place whence it overflowed into Arabia and the outside world.

English enterprise has never yet done justice by equatorial Africa. Small quantities of Coffee are grown along the eastern coast, in Abyssinia, the Somali country, Mozambique, Madagascar, Natal, Reunion, and Mauritius; but the total yield, so far as its influence upon the supply of Europe and the United States is concerned, is insignificant, as the export capacity of all the places named did not lately exceed from 600 to 800 tons annually. The product of the eastern provinces of Africa, taken in connection with the small crops raised on the west coast, makes Africa contribute between 3,000 and 4,000 tons to the world's production, the amount including Coffee grown in Egypt and the interior countries of the continent; and this simply means that the Coffee growing (except perhaps in the extreme south) is all done by natives, and Ceylon planters will know what this means.

The following letter, written especially for this chapter by one of the most popular of those explorers who are rapidly opening up the "Dark Continent," will be read with interest:—

COFFEE IN AFRICA.

"The Coffee plant is one of the few useful economic products that the African flora has as yet given to the world. The genus Coffœa divided into many species is practically indigenous to the African continent, for the wild Coffee in Arabia only inhabits the mountain slopes of the western shore of that peninsula where it faces the African mainland. Whilst Coffee grows wild over most parts of tropical Africa, its cultivation in the Dark Continent is very slight and partial at present, although it offers a future of boundless development. Almost the only part of Africa that I know of wherein Coffee planting is carried on by the natives of the soil, and not by aliens of European or Arabian descent, is Northern Angola. It is possible that here the idea sprang originally from Portuguese tuition, but, nevertheless, in many districts lying between the Lower Congo and Angola, wherein no white man has yet penetrated, Coffee planting and gathering is carried on by the natives, who bring their harvests down to the coast at Ambrig and neighbouring settlements to sell to the white (principally French) traders.

"The Portuguese colonists of Angola, São Thorné, and Principe plant Coffee largely, and their products are high in value. At the Gaboon the French missionaries have tried with some success to introduce Coffee planting. The Americanized Negroes of Liberia cultivate lazily and half-heartedly some of the fine local species, such as C. Liberiensis. I think a little desultory planting goes on in Sierra Leone and the Gambia Colonies. The French are doing a great deal in Senegal. The Coffee plant grows wild in the Congo region, and the districts round Glanlypool are eminently suited to its cultivation, but as yet no one has commenced any Coffee planting, and the natives of these countries, unlike the Negroes farther south towards Angola, ignore the properties of the Coffee berry.

"I believe something is done in Natal and a good deal is going to be done on the Zambesi. Usambara, opposite Zanzibar, is a glorious field for Coffee planting — admirable soil, peaceable inhabitants, cheap labour (from the Zanzibar labour market), and land to be had for next to nothing. The missionaries of the Universities' Mission are distributing the Coffee berry among the inhabitants to induce them to cultivate it. Transport is easy, and the distance from the coast and good ports a matter of one to two days' journey. Further into the interior there are increasingly fine sites and suitable soil for Coffee planting, only owned as yet by the birds of the air and the beasts of the field. The writer has planted Coffee on and at the base of Mount Kilimanjaro, and from six months' experience finds the young plants thrive wonderfully.

"Farther north, in Somaliland, Coffee is everywhere wild, but apparently remains uncultivated by man. This rapid survey of Africa brings us back to Southern Abyssinia and the country of Kaffa, where Coffee first began to be cultivated and introduced to the world.

"The best fields for Coffee planting in Africa known to the writer are the Usambara, Pare, and Kilimanjaro districts (where efficient and cheap labour may be procured close at hand in Zanzibar); the Zambesi and the Nyassa district, Angola, São Thorné, and Principe—all Portuguese possessions, where land is exceedingly cheap and life and property are secure; the Congo districts, the Gold Coast, and the Gambia, but the two latter districts are well populated by aborigines and are exceedingly unhealthy for Europeans.

"The writer is convinced that Kilimanjaro and the surrounding country offers almost the finest opening for Coffee planting in Africa. It is sparsely populated, near the coast, endowed with a perfect climate and singularly fertile soil."

Coffee at the Cape might have succeeded, but "the Kaffirs will not work in Natal," we read in "A South African Sketch Book" (Sonnenschein)—

"Coolie labour is too expensive, and English labour cannot be retained. Thus Coffee cannot be said, in any sense, to have flourished well in the colony. In the sub-tropical climate of Natal, the plant buds, flowers, and develops its berries in the most erratic manner all the year round. Double, if not treble, labour is necessary in the selection of the fruit; in short, it has to be gathered two or three times over. Coffee bears its berries in this most inconvenient fashion. The unhappy grower whose trees are budding, flowering, and bearing all at the same moment is placed on the horns of a dilemma. Either he must sacrifice much of his crop, or else he must submit to two outlays in the way of labour. This is a very awkward position to be in, in that labour is not only expensive, but often absolutely unprocurable. The Kaffirs, who are under monthly terms of engagement, are as likely as not to leave one at a most critical juncture, when fine crops must be gathered or perish. This has too often proved disastrous to the prospects of the Coffee and sugar planters. What kind of luck would our hop farmers call it if, in addition to all the other risks to which they are exposed, they were finally checkmated entirely, by having to whistle for labour when the burr had become fully ripe and ready to be gathered in? The Natalians have imported coolie labour, which is far more reliable than the so-called aboriginal labour, to meet the difficulty. But coolie labour is expensive, in that the importer has to pay the passage money of his servant from India to Natal, and back again. The coolie is bound for three years only, and it so happens that the unfortunate employer, who cannot with all his prescience be expected to see so far into futurity, is often compelled to dispense with the services of the coolies, and let them return home, when he most imperatively requires their services.

"There is plenty of soil favourable to the growth of Coffee in Natal, but it is not always to be found in a convenient spot, that is to say, near the coast."

Liberia is the home of a famous variety, said to be fairly proof against the leaf disease. For foreigners it is exceedingly difficult to set an enterprise on foot. The Liberians cede no land in fee-simple to whites, they at most lease it out for forty years. Besides this, the white man would soon suffer from the prevailing agues, and so have to leave a great deal to the care of a coloured manager.

Formerly it was supposed that the Liberia Coffee-tree, which exceeds all other known sorts in size, was either introduced from India, or centuries ago by the Portuguese. It is now generally held to be of native growth, on account of its never attaining its original size when transplanted elsewhere, and that it is never found in any other part of Africa. It is found only between 4° to 7° north latitude, and it grows spontaneously from the seacoast to the luxurious grassy plains of Abandingo Land.

The climate of Liberia seems unequalled for

the culture of Coffee. The temperature varies in the shade from 74° to 80° Fahrenheit, but rises in the dry season from 90° to far beyond 100°; the lowest point, 62° at sunrise, was observed at Monravia in January, during the prevalence of the harmattan-winds. The difference in the interior is not so great, because the ground rises so rapidly; 25 miles from the coast the land is already 500 feet, and at a distance of 198 miles as much as 2,200 feet above the level of the sea. Yet the Coffee is everywhere the same. Even in a wild state, there are splendid trees from 10 to 12 inches in diameter; the cultivated plants are not much smaller. For laying out a plantation, the best land would be a wooded, rocky, hilly country, a few miles from the seashore; there are found those loose loamy soils, with a rocky ground and the manure of decayed leaves, which are the most appropriate. The water absorbed by the porous ground keeps, even in the dry season, the Coffee tree fresh and verdant. A sandy soil with a bottom of a few feet of loam would also do very well.

Liberian Coffee has also been cultivated since 1880 in the Seychelles; the first plants were sent from Kew and distributed among a few planters by Mr. C. S. Salmon, then Chief Civil Commissioner. They grew very rapidly, and those planted in proper soil, and entirely exposed to the sun, began to bear before two years old; while others in rich ground, and at a short distance from other trees, grew with more vigour, but only began to bear long after. It has been propagated in different localities, and everywhere seems to prefer an open situation, where it bears abundantly. The quantity lately planted may amount to about 100 acres.

www.ingramcontent.com/pod-product-compliance
Lightning Source LLC
Chambersburg PA
CBHW031929230426
43672CB00010B/1865